TELECITY

TELECITY

Information Technology
and Its Impact
on City Form

Tarik A. Fathy

PRAEGER

New York
Westport, Connecticut
London

Library of Congress Cataloging-in-Publication Data

Fathy, Tarik A.
    Telecity : information technology and its impact on city form /
Tarik A. Fathy.
        p.   cm.
    Includes bibliographical references (p.   ) and index.
    ISBN 0-275-93814-X (alk. paper)
        1. Cities and towns—Forecasting.   2. Information technology—
Social aspects—Forecasting.   3. City planning.   I. Title.
HT153.F37   1991
307.76—dc20   91-443

British Library Cataloguing in Publication Data is available.

Library of Congress Catalog Card Number: 91-443
ISBN: 0-275-93814-X

First published in 1991

Praeger Publishers, One Madison Avenue, New York, NY 10010
An imprint of Greenwood Publishing Group, Inc.

Printed in the United States of America

The paper used in this book complies with the
Permanent Paper Standard issued by the National
Information Standards Organization (Z39.48—1984).

10 9 8 7 6 5 4 3 2 1

To Sherine
　　　　To my parents and brothers
　　　　　　　And to our future, Amr and Saja

Contents

Illustrations

FIGURES

TABLES

Preface

This book examines the impact of technology on city form and structure. Several studies on the social impact of technology have already been conducted, each from a different viewpoint. However, the real question has not yet been asked.

The main concern of this book is the relationship between socioeconomic activities and the transformation process of existing cities in modern societies accelerated by the emerging information revolution. The study proceeds through the development of concepts based on virtual networks of communication to perform new types of social activities. The concepts of the telecity and teleactivities occupy integral roles in the study.

My audience consists essentially of scholars and designers. Scholars may be interested in the development of the main concept of telecity emerging from the analysis of new socioeconomic relationships. While critically relating different theoretical perspectives to the analysis and findings, they find this study pursues its objectives using an uncommon approach—its research acts as a confirmatory exercise to the central concepts. Designers, on the other hand, have an interest in the potential of new information technologies. The introduction of new tools provides insights for better solutions to city problems, and the articulated structures in chapter 6 would initiate discussions on the image and functions of future cities. I must emphasize here that the telecity concept is neither a rigid metaphor nor a solution to every urban area. This book is an attempt to assist both audiences to understand the current changing environment and provides challenging propositions on the relationship of new information technologies to city form.

Acknowledgments

This study could never have developed or been completed without the valuable contributions of many people. My learning experience at Cairo University, Faculty of Engineering, Architectural Department, has opened my mind to the fascinating field of urban planning. Through the teachings of M. Yousri Hasan, the powers of planning in its social and cultural context have been understood and appreciated. Without the academic insights and support of Sayyed Ettouny, who eloquently linked physical planning to social theory, my journey to the United States would have been more difficult.

At the University of Southern California, the liberal academic atmosphere allowed this study to mature into its present form. I would like to acknowledge the invaluable contributions of my U.S.C. professors and colleagues, especially Manuel Castells, who has helped define the scope of this study during his spring visits to Los Angeles.

Valuable assistance came from the Center for Telecommunications Management at U.S.C. in developing the questionnaire, reviewing the data base to locate panelists, and proceeding with the Delphi exercise, making our work much easier. Special thanks to Masoud Saghafi for his willing cooperation and cheerful support.

The contributions of the panelists were the essence of sustaining the view of this study.

A very grateful admiration to Tridib Banerjee, Everett Rogers, and Omar El-Sawy, who all introduced me to new fields of knowledge and provided general wisdom and insights. Their critical views, challenging ideas, and endless encouragement sailed me safely in the course of the study when it was greatly needed.

My dearest respect and gratitude goes to my mentor Lowdon Wingo. Without his endless support and gracious understanding this work would never be completed. I am deeply indebted to his scholarly teachings, sharp arguments, and generous kindness. His knowledge and intuition navigated my turbulent ideas to shores of competence and coherence, his encouragement and inspiration paved many hurdles in times of despair, and his vision and wisdom insured the completion of this study.

This book is dedicated to my family. I strongly feel that this work would reward the memory of my father, whose discipline, love, and kindness allowed me to believe in unattainable ends. His study and career always energize me to try to achieve what he effortlessly accomplished forty years ago. The emotional support and frequent trips are extremely appreciated from a strong loving mother. Her continuous assurances upheld the course of my study. My elder brother, Essam, has to carry the burden of managing my stay in the United States for a long time. It is always certain who I can lean on. My twin brother, colleague, and friend lent his tremendous input and critical views to this study. Being my classmate gave both of us a sense of competition, compassion, and sharing. Hisham and I created an atmosphere that allowed both of us to perform and deliver. His input to this study is the most appreciated. A special thanks for the graceful love, caring, and patience of my wife, Sherine, who sacrificed many years to complete this work. She deserves hearty praise and grateful indebtedness for illuminating moments of despondency. Finally, this work is for my nephew, Amr, and my beloved baby daughter, Saja, to set a humble example of hard work. Above all, my humble submission to God whose blessings are innumerous.

TELECITY

1

Introduction

CITIES OF THE FUTURE

Since the dawn of civilization, cities have been the communication and information centers of their societies. Various means of communication permit concentration of activities to exchange ideas efficiently, facilitate transactions, and transfer information, which set the boundaries between villages and cities. The larger the city, the more sophisticated are its communication networks.[1]

Until the nineteenth century all communications were greatly impeded by distance and limited to direct verbal speech. Communication and travel were synonymous, and communication channels overlay transportation networks in the form of roads, waterways, and later, railroads. Transportation innovations, such as the tramway and automobile, and new communication channels, such as the telephone, began the conquest of the distance barrier and have altered both the speed and location of interaction. Increased mobility permitted expansion of city boundaries, dispersion of residential landscape, and location of industry.

Since the mid-1970s, new information technologies have increasingly become the means of interactive communication among people scattered throughout the world. Today the telephone has become more than a luxury item or household convenience; it is a fundamental form of interpersonal communication. Following the same trends, television, cable networks, and personal computers have increasingly become part of our everyday life.

Social scientists have recognized the potential of low-cost communication facilities to increase accessibility. They have viewed transportation and communication as the central assets of urban areas. Wingo (1961) contends that technological changes alter the "movement demand" in urban areas, and an even greater accessibility lies in society's ability to substitute communication for transportation, to replace the movement of goods and persons with the transmission of information. Furthermore, Meier (1962), Webber (1963a), and Mandelbaum (1972) address the important potential of substituting communication for transportation by studying the effect of nearly zero transportation cost on urban growth. Emergence of the current technological revolution has dramatically reduced the cost of interactive communications (Williams 1982). Notions of global village, electronic cottage, and wired city have become common in the literature, which reflect the worldwide interconnectedness by means of new information technologies.

As information sources became more essential and remote, the use and application of communication technologies have become vital to sustaining socioeconomic activities. In the information society, telecommunications—the functional integration of communication channels and computers—have become strategic elements to generate, process, manage, and control information (Beniger 1986).

The current technological advancement plays an important role in reshaping urban forms and structures through socioeconomic processes. These changes are a response to: (1) the restructuring of the labor market in favor of international division of labor and demand for highly skilled occupations (Bell 1973; Singh 1977; Sabel 1982; Stroper and Walker 1984); (2) the changing of location of industry and business marketplace (Greenhut 1971; Dordick et al. 1979; Farely and Glickman 1986; Markusen et al. 1986); and (3) the shifting toward services and information-based activities (Castells 1976; Gershuny 1978, 1983; Stanback 1979; Faulhaber et al. 1986). These transformation processes have affected nearly all aspects of American urban life. Contemporary debates in urban planning reflect an escalation of general tensions and conflicts that include: growth limits of metropolitan areas (Sawers and Tabb 1984; Gottmann 1977; Dear and Scott 1981; Thwaites and Oakey 1985); traffic problems and congestion (Erlander 1977; Brotchie 1984; Wachs 1984); urban renewal of central business districts (CBDs) (Castells 1983a, 1984); decentralization of economic activity (Golany 1976; Greene 1980; Moss 1986); development of public transportation policies (Henderson 1975; Lake 1983; Simpson 1987); the location decisions for traditional and new high-tech industries (Glasmeier 1985; Markusen et al. 1986; Saxenian 1984); and the ecological concerns on preserving rural areas against suburban expansion.

The study of technology's impact on urban life, however, is still in its infancy.[2] Only recently have social scientists recognized the importance of this branch of social inquiry (Fleisher 1960; Golany 1976; Pool 1977; Teich 1981; Castells 1985; Brotchie et al. 1985; Forester 1985). Their studies have been dominated by three views. The first claim suggests that dramatic changes already in progress will transform every aspect of our lives including shape and structure of city form (Toffler 1970, 1980; Webber 1973; Naisbitt 1982; Williams 1982; Moss 1986); a second claim argues that if there are any changes, they will be minor at city scale. Changes occur in industrial location decisions, specifically in high-tech industries, in the urban–regional restructuring process at the geographical level (Malecki 1983; Castells 1985; Glasmeier 1985; Markusen et al. 1986; Wachs 1984).[3] The third claim focuses only on the information revolution in individual business and corporations. Many concepts and facilities, including cable television, VCRs, satellite broadcasting, videotext, teletext, and online services, are affecting organizations and firms by changing market and production economics, the division of labor, and products and services. This claim suggests adopting new information technologies and developing new organizational structures to accommodate the new changing conditions of the economic survival of business (Tavel 1975; Nilles 1984; Nanus 1982; Compaine 1984; El-Sawy 1985; Porter 1985; Cross and Raizman 1986).

These views are inadequate. The first is a technological determinism, which neglects the fact that social processes of adoption and diffusion of innovations are gradual, not dramatic (Rogers

1983). New communication technologies alone cannot alter city form—they are part of larger socioeconomic processes. Inventions are neither revolutions nor the cause of revolutions. They only can offer new freedom of action by removing old constraints (Cherry 1977). "Regionalists," on the other hand, overlook the impact of technology. They limit the effect of new information technologies to industrial and business location decisions without considering the impact on other urban activities. Moreover, by focusing only on the production of specialized geographical centers of high-tech industries, regionalists negate technological impact on social values and individual preference. The third view, "reductionism," does not explain the aggregate impact of changing organizations and their workplaces on urban life. They neglect the fact that individual business activities and services collectively influence urban centers and locational patterns, and that broader social issues determine organization behavior.

This study seeks to repair these inadequacies on impact of new information technologies on urban life in the information society. It establishes a theoretical framework emerging from three city form perspectives to integrate the consequences of new information technologies on the city physical elements; the dynamics of economic activities and location decisions; and the interpretation processes of city social meaning.

The main concern of this study is the relationship between socioeconomic forces of social change and the physical transformation process of the existing city in Western countries. I will focus on the influence of technology as the most critical socioeconomic force. That does not mean technology is an autonomous or deterministic factor, but rather an analytical element in order to investigate which form of the city accommodates these social changes and which structure appropriates them.[4] The complexity of the social impact of technology and the broad interests of many disciplines in technological change foreshadow an innovative approach that establishes a concept to elucidate the influence of the current social transformation events and their forms in urban life.

This study argues that the revolution in the use and application of information produces a "telecity." This telecity concept implies that a critical mass of inhabitants in a geographical landscape are engaged in interactive communication networks where remote services, facilities, and work dominate city life. It engages the changing characteristics of the contemporary American city. The telecity demands a multinodal, nonhierarchical structure to accommodate layers of "teleactivities," which are socioeconomic activities based on interactive, individualized, and asynchronous communication systems to connect persons, tasks, and information regardless of their actual locations. Online economies (networks of information services), teleworking (working at home for one or more days per week using microcomputers that are connected to the home office computer systems), and psychological neighborhoods (a mental landscape to connect a virtual structure of activities depending on each individual interactive communication with work, shop, entertainment, and social relations) are emerging types of teleactivities. Linear physical movement on city transportation systems is complemented by superimposed multidimensional mobility on virtual networks.

The telecity concept is the central theme of this study. It is based on: (1) the superimposition of virtual networks of activities, made possible by the application of new information technologies and the shift toward information-based activities; and (2) the existing physical form of the city. It depends on interpretation and personalization processes of the telecity inhabitants in relation to both the spatial and temporal structure of the city. In fact, telecity began with the introduction of the two-way communication network (telephone), but the new forms of telecommunications and the high adoption rate of personal computers have paved the way for more extensive uses of this technology in a variety of everyday activities.

The telecity concept differs from earlier concepts and should not be judged by their success or failure. The telecity is not a wired city. Wired cities are experimental projects that implement highly sophisticated two-way cable television networks and other new information technologies (Dutton et al. 1988). Ten communities have already entertained these systems in more than five countries—the United States, England, France, Japan, and Germany. A wired city is basically a small-scale community, artificially implemented, not indigenous evolution of socioeconomic forces, and individuals are not necessarily engaged in work types that call for disassociation of the worker and his traditional workplace. Since it is still in its early stages, objectively evaluating its outcome would be difficult.

On the other hand, the telecity is not a technopolis. Technopolis is a specialized community in which an industrial sector, particularly high-tech, is dominant (Simlor et al. 1988). It is a concentration of a high-tech industrial complex located in a favorable area close to research centers and universities with strong ties to governmental agencies such as the Defense Department, for the development of industry (Rogers and Valente 1988). But the concept of the telecity applies to any existing cities in Western societies in their transformation processes.

The research, however, requires a multidisciplinary approach that conceptually combines diverse impacts of technology. Technological inquiry belongs to a class of problems in the social sciences demanding a logic more complex than that of simple causality. Thus, the task of this study is not to specify cause–effect relationships but to identify transformation processes and their spatial development, providing new ways of thinking about the future.

This study is about information technologies and city form. *City form* is the spatial arrangement of society, the spatial structure and flow of persons, goods, and information, and the physical features that modify space in ways significant to those actions (including enclosures, surfaces, channels, ambience, and objects) (Lynch 1984, 345). *New information technologies* are those telecommunication systems that depend on interactive, individualized, and asynchronous networks. These systems are the result of rapid changes in applying new concepts and innovations in the use of information (Rogers 1985). *Information* is the patterned matter-energy that affects the probabilities of decision making and reduces uncertainty (Rogers 1985).[5]

This study has two central objectives. First, it establishes the relationship between technology and city form. Current events suggest modification in city form as a result of changes in new information technologies that feed social transformation process toward information-based activities, and, in return, demand further development in information technology. This analysis pursues socioeconomic relationships that generate new types of activities liberated from time and distance limitations. The aggregation of these remote activities (teleactivities) produces the telecity.

Second, this study analyzes the telecity concept to anticipate changes in major assumptions of theories of city forms. The telecity concept is a template to render changes from different perspectives: the physicalist, the urban economist, and the sociologist. The telecity concept acts as a magnifier to explain city form from integrated viewpoints.

ORGANIZATION OF THE STUDY

The structure of this study reflects its two objectives, whose argument advances through six chapters. After the introduction, chapter 2 examines the inadequate views about technology. It explains its relationship to science, its conception, and its historical evolution. The chapter follows the development of industrial societies and critically analyzes the role of technology by addressing three schools of thought: the subjective, the cost-of-production, and the labor theories of value. It challenges the conventional theories of industrial production that technology is capital intensive versus labor. The changing nature of current technologies reveals misleading ideas about technology while unveiling its interpretive dimension. This chapter concludes by establishing a way of understanding technology and its impact on society.

Chapter 3 describes the current social transformation into an information society. To investigate the new role of information technologies, it provides a production-consumption model of society. It attempts to map production activities in an information society by its leading sectors of information, traditional industries, and high-tech production. Then, it relates production activities to the diffusion of new information technologies. New information technologies are categorized according to their impact on various aspects of city form: infrastructure and hardware; communication channels and operation systems; and information services and software. The dialectical interaction between production and consumption activities involving new information technologies results in the emergence of new multilevel remote activities. The aggregation of teleactivities transforms the existing cities in information societies into telecities. This chapter establishes the telecity concept and its characteristics.

Chapter 4 introduces a new research technique to deal with the future. A Delphi exercise is applied to reflect the potential of social transformation processes likely to occur within a domain of change expectations. This technique emphasizes a dynamic process that includes judgmental data from a wide array of experts. Results of this exercise validate the propositions introduced in chapter 3 concerning the emergence of teleactivities, their consequences, and the rate of their social acceptance and diffusion. It is a confirmatory probe into the emergence of the telecity concept.

Chapter 5 deals with theories of city form from three main perspectives to elucidate characteristics of the telecity concept. First, the physicalist perspective emphasizes the physical components of city reflected in perception processes and, hence, in the images of the city. Second, the urban economic perspective refers to location decisions and the resultant relationship of land uses and transportation systems. Third, the social meaning perspective considers the city as a manifestation of the symbolic environment. Three theories are introduced in the third perspective: social meaning as conflicting interests of historically determined powers (Castells 1983a, 1983b), situational behavior theory of diffusion of communication media and technology (Meyrowitz 1985; Rogers 1983), and social order of interpreted culture (Rapoport 1969, 1984). These perspectives expound new dimensions of the telecity concept manifested in a multinodal, nonhierarchical structure with superimposed multidimensional mobility on virtual networks.

Chapter 6 presents configurations of the telecity in several distributed structures. It proposes linkages between spatial and temporal structures, which suggest relationships among physical patterns and superimposed networks. Four different layers are generated based on the new information technologies' locational, virtual, and temporal characteristics, which are: (1) the transportation networks and communication systems, (2) service location, (3) topological distribution, and (4) technological structure.

Then, it concludes the impact of new information technologies and the emergence of telecity concept by proposing four public policy implications. The study suggests standardization and deregulation policies of new information technologies infrastructure, the reconsideration of land use regulation and zoning, and public investment in conventional infrastructure policies to reflect changes in work activity and its relation to residential areas. Far from being comprehensive, this study concludes by recommending directions for further studies.

NOTES

1. In villages, networks tend to be overlapping, comprehensive, and in that sense closed, whereas in cities they are nonoverlapping and open-ended toward variety, diversity of interests, and pluralistic standards and styles (Keller 1977, 283). Also see Marx and Engels (1977).

2. Few studies focus on technological consequences for the city. Mostly, brief statements are interspersed in the literature. Generally, these statements are projections into the future, based on fragile assumptions of what the writers believe (Gottmann 1977).

3. The "California Group" are researchers sharing similar viewpoints on new socioeconomic conditions. They wrote a series of studies at the University of California, Berkeley. Their work has appeared in a number of working papers of the Institute of Urban and Regional Development at Berkeley, and in several books such as *High Technology, Space and Society* and *High-Tech America*. They are fundamentally involved in studying the new space of production and industrial location decisions on the regional scale, without any attention to the dynamics of city scale.

4. Several one-dimensional or partial views on the relationship between technological change and society have been advanced. Technology is seen by some as an autonomous force developed according to its own internal laws. Others see it as an almost unmitigated curse: technology is said to rob people of their jobs, their privacy, their values and beliefs. The third view, which tends to be held by historians for whom continuity is an indispensable assumption, considers technology unworthy of special attention. They argue that improved communications and education (fundamentally technological) are responses to society's technological changes, and that rate of technological adoption is roughly in equilibrium with man's social and psychological development (Mesthene 1970).

5. For elaborate discussion on information entropy and uncertainty, refer to Campbell, *Grammatical Man* (1982). Information lacks a physical existence of its own and can only be expressed in material form (on paper, magnetic tapes, discs) or in energy form (electrical impulses). Because information is such an abstract phenomenon, its crucial importance in modern societies is not easily apparent (Rogers 1985).

2

Technology and Society

Since the Stone Age, civilizations have been characterized by the type of technology they use, and it has always played a role in the transformation of urban form. It is a dynamic force of change in urban life because its advances impose alterations in city structure and systems (Mumford 1961; Benevolo 1971; Morris 1972). Improvements in basic infrastructure, such as the introduction of sewage systems and water supply networks in Greco-Roman cities, altered building arrangements and urban patterns, and therefore, urban environment.

In the industrial city, the generation of electrical power brought about major changes. The new form of energy created new machinery and manufacturing techniques for mass production in large factories. It extended daytime activities past sunset. It made possible new modes of transportation—the tramway, which dispersed social activities into wider areas and enlarged the pool of labor around larger units of industrial production.[1] Electricity enabled the invention of the elevator and the telephone. The elevator, with the use of new materials such as steel and concrete, reshaped the structure of urban components and altered city skyline. Highrise buildings allowed concentrations of activities in the city center, while telephone networks interlinked businesses in congested city centers in large metropolitan areas.[2]

Then the motorcar radically altered accessibility among residents, materials, and markets. It broke down the existing pedestrian network patterns (Mumford 1961). Cities grew in size and population to merge with adjacent cities, creating a "megalopolis" such as those around New York, London, or Los Angeles. Invention of the motorcar was the prime factor in development of suburbs, satellite towns, and residential expansion at the growing edge of most metropolitan areas (Clawson 1971).[3] New street patterns to suit the dominant mode of transportation with heavy expenditures for construction, operation, and maintenance for highways, roads, and traffic control developed to facilitate movement from one part of the city to another (Wingo 1963).

The influence of technology, however, is not limited to the introduction of new materials, machines, or transportation modes, but more fundamentally, the introduction of new activities of production and consumption (Castells 1977, 21). From the founding of cities, development of human knowledge and technology created specialized work, which established the division of material and mental labor in the separation between town and country. The country produced agricultural goods while the city accommodated most social, commercial, tool making, and religious activities (Mumford 1961; Marx and Engels 1977). Technology served as an extension to muscle power and a counterpart to manual effort in agricultural societies.[4]

At the heart of the Industrial Revolution, which completely transformed Western life-style in a span of one century, lay a cluster of new technologies, energy resources, modes of transportation, innovative techniques, and modes of industrial production. Most important, the organization of work in large, centrally powered units (factories and mills) made possible more efficient, low-cost, standardized products with higher degree of division of labor in a competitive labor market (Mumford 1961; Goldthrope 1984).

The labor market was structured in relation to the industrial mode of production, which was dominated by two kinds of firms. The first kind depends on a sizable and stable demand for its products and mass market growth. These firms have invested in technological innovations that reduce production costs and redistribute skills among workers. A few had jobs requiring sophisticated knowledge; the rest (a majority) were assigned to routine specialized tasks. In 1913 Ford's Highland Park, Michigan, plant with its automobile assembly line became the climax of the push toward standardization of products and production. Sabel (1982) uses the "Fordism Model" as a shorthand term for the organizational and technological principles of the modern large-scale factory.

The second kind of firm was smaller, faced fluctuating demand, and lived in the shadow of the first. It pursued short-term investment strategies requiring less specialized use of labor and often employed technologies discarded by the larger firms. These "backward" firms were primarily in repair and maintenance businesses.[5]

The impact of technology on socioeconomic conditions of society was perceived by three competing schools of thought: the subjective preference theory of value, the cost-of-production theory of value, and the abstract labor theory of value. Each was concerned with technology's impact on socioeconomic activities as a way of understanding the valuation of human activity (Cole et al. 1983). (See table 2.1.)

The *subjective preference theory of value* is based on a tradition started by Jevons, Menger, and Walras in the late nineteenth century, developed by Pareto and Fisher in the first half of this century, and then elaborated by Friedman (1953), Brittan (1975), and Arrow (1963). This school views technology as an autonomous development in a self-contained political and economic system. It suggests that the individual is endowed with tastes and talents and calculates actions to maximize his or her welfare (utility) in a free market (Cole et al. 1983) where tastes define preferences among alternative consumption patterns, and talents determine the ability to fulfill these desires through productive activity, which is increased by specialization (i.e., division of labor). For this school, technology reduces prices for higher consumption through mass production and substituting machines for labor, and allows the individual to apply talents to division of labor (entrepreneurship). Due to the apparent sepa-

Table 2.1
Summary of the Dominant Paradigms of Political Economy in Industrial Society

FEATURE	DOMINANT PARADIGM OF POLITICAL ECONOMY		
SCHOOLS	Subjective Preference	Cost of Production	Abstract Labor
Determination of Value	Individual Utility: in Consumption	Technology Distribution in production	Social Relations: Historic
Political Conflict	No Conflict in Free Exchange	Conflict over Distribution	Conflict Fundamental to Society
Political Institutions	Representative	Pluralist	Class Power
Theory of Social Change	Gradual: Development of New Ideas	Evolutionary: Technology Development	Revolutionary: Class Struggle
Role of Technology	Autonomous	Determinist	Structure to Superstructure
Misleading Ideas	DETERMINISM + REDUCTIONISM + ESSENTIALISM		
New Conditions	EMERGENCE OF INFORMATION SOCIETY		

Source: Based on Cole, Cameron, and Edward (1983).

ration between the individual as consumer and the individual as producer, society is the aggregate of various individuals engaged in activities of production and consumption.

The *cost-of-production theory of value*, which originated in the works of Veblen (1932) and Marshall (1947), was elaborated by Keynes (1936) and Chamberlin (1933), and developed in its current stage by Robinson (1933), Sraffa (1960), and Galbraith (1958), proposes that value is determined by decisions to produce, rather than decisions to consume. The prevailing technology dictates the nature and method of production, and therefore determines the technical division of labor, which in turn necessitates exchange of products at exchange rates (prices) based on each good's cost of production including distribution of social product between wages and profits.

In this theory, technology plays a deterministic role in production. Since everyone depends on others in the technical division of labor, the temporal equilibrium of political-economic forces of ever-changing interest groups is threatened by technological change. Thus, there is a possibility of sectional opposition to the introduction of new techniques. Technology, it is argued, must be tamed, if the accelerative thrust is to be brought under control (Winner 1977).

The third school, *labor theory of value*, emerges from the Marxist tradition where material environment is transformed through production of goods that individuals wish to use. The type of technology employed, as in cost-of-production theory, determines the technical division of labor; but it is based upon a relationship of power over the means of production. The entire structure of production, distribution, exchange, and consumption reflects social relations of production (Sweezy 1939; Fine 1975).

Marx (1970), in his view of historical development, defines the industrial mode of production (economic structure of society) as the "techniques of production and technical knowledge concerned with the development and use of resources." The mode of production (the base structure in his terms) affects social institutions and social relations. Its influence on superstructure (ideology, state, and social institutions) is the basic line of causation in history. Technology (human productive forces) initiates a change in relation of production, and therefore, it has a determining role in human history (Elliott 1985).

So far these three schools share a basic concept that the economic growth process is essentially a profit-investment-technology model. The growth rate in potential output depends on resources (capital, land, and labor) and technology. Technology is seen as capital investment. By increasing labor productivity and decreasing costs, technological improvements raise the potential output and profit for further investment. Therefore, the profitability of investment depends on consumption as well as technology. In comparison, employment, the sources of wage income, and consumption depend on the relation between the flow of investment and technology (the stock of labor-saving capital innovations) (Elliott, 1985).

The previous theories of industrialism failed to explain the role of technology in the new socioeconomic conditions of modern society. They limited technology to three fundamental misleading ideas: technological determinism, essentialism, and reductionism (Sabel 1982).

First, technological determinism stands on two hypotheses: (1) the technical base of a society is the fundamental condition affecting all patterns of social existence, and (2) technological changes are the single most important source of change in society (Winner 1977). Any society that wants to produce industrial goods must adopt specific models of organization, patterns of authority, and techniques of conducting business.

The objection to technological determinism is that the performance standards can be met in several ways. The fit between what needs to be done and how it can be done is seldom as tight as the determinists imagine. Plants using comparable technologies can divide the necessary work in various ways while the same goods can be produced via different technologies. For example, the Ford Motor Company is one of many firms that owns and operates factories in different countries. Despite the similarities among these factories in terms of ample access to technological knowledge, capital, engineers, production facilities, and products manufactured, the technology in use is different. The technology that factories are using in Detroit (much more powered equipment for each worker) differs from the technology factories use in Dagenham, England. One factor, relative cost of labor versus machinery, is responsible for the variation in technology in the two countries (Melman et al. 1972).

Second, essentialism, an offspring of determinism, is the claim that what is true for society as a whole is true for its parts. The more advanced an industrial society, the more clearly modern forms of organization predominate in each of its parts. As a result, the differences between industrial societies disappear, each becoming more internally homogeneous.

The objection to essentialism is that radically different forms of organization are often interdependent. Advances in some industries create preconditions for the survival of outdated forms of industrial organization. The existence of the "backward" small firms is sometimes essential for the survival of large industrial organizations to meet flexible demand for maintenance and repair.

Third, reductionism is the doctrine that "experience determines thought." Consequently, everyday experience in modern societies determines the aspirations and desires of those societies' members. Reductionists argue that human wants are not fixed, but rather change over time, stimulated by society's capacity to satisfy them. The development of technology, for example, produces new goods that awaken new needs and desires, spurring further technological advances, and so on the cycle continues (Sabel 1982). Thus, industrialization means the end of ideology. If industrialization produces a uniform experience of life, and if the experience produces agreement that technology should be efficiently used to satisfy wants, ideologies have lost their significance (Bell 1967).

The objection to reductionism is that technological development is usually shaped by social choices imposed through the political structure or the market. For example, changing oil prices and environmental concerns have forced changes in automobile design (Sabel 1982).

The mode of production does not unify societies. Cultural differences have not disappeared, and the same forces of production exist within a variety of different systems of social relations (Bell 1973). Any society, since it mingles different kinds of social, economic, political, and technological systems (even though some features are common to all), has to be analyzed from different angles, depending on the context.

While in principle all technology is subject to human control (Goodwin 1981), Ellul (1980) argues that technology is an autonomous force with the power to influence institutions and cultures, thus affecting the traditional values of every society without exception. Still, technology is a neutral tool that, as part of the social process will change values and social relations only when broader social changes occur (Boguslaw 1972).

The current progress in technology foreshadows a powerful shift of understanding about its role in social transformation.[6] The information revolution exposes a new dimension of technology revealing hidden characteristics. A study of philosophical foundations of technology is essential to explain the misleading ideas about technology.

CONCEPTION OF TECHNOLOGY

Despite roots extending back to classical Greece, the systematic study of technology as a special branch of human activity is a modern phenomenon. Technology, the combination of "techne" (art, craft) and "logos" (word, study), means the discourse on the arts, both fine and applied. As a tool-making animal, *homo faber*, man has achieved great advances through the relationship of science and technology.

Science in the classical world belonged to the aristocratic philosophers and embodied all knowledge, while technology was the possession of the working craftsmen. "True" science was an intellectual activity devoid of laboratory experimentation and disciplined observation (LeVine 1984). It was inwardly focused, separated from the concern of the everyday world, and contained little or no understanding of the workings of nature. Theory was completely separate from practice, while science was thought to be conducted for the general purpose of expanding our understanding of nature so that we may ultimately improve our welfare (Merton 1957; Barber 1962). On the other hand, the status of artisans engaged in more mechanistic and instrumental activity was considered far below the status of scientists (Solomon 1973, 10).

During the Renaissance scientists took new notice of the ancient crafts and advocated a closer relationship with them. Trade led to the development of fine arts and artisans, technicians, and craftsmen. The arts, it was suggested, could provide problems for science to solve, while science might provide laws and rules that could allow the arts to progress more rapidly. In the sixteenth century Francis Bacon advanced the view that scientists should study the craftsman's methods and the craftsmen should acquire more scientific knowledge. He envisioned no division between the instrumental nature of science and its usefulness in human service. Knowledge and action were inseparable and necessary in order to conquer nature in the interest of public service (Solomon 1973). Bacon strongly influenced the evolution of the present understanding of science, which is but a "socially conditioned enterprise" (Haberer 1969, 31).[7]

The French Revolution for the first time forced "pure" scientists to work on practical problems whose solutions would yield immediate benefits to political institutions. It organized scientists specifically for counseling the state on technical (military) matters. It cast science as a tool of the state by its relation to technology by removing it from the realm of theory and focusing on its practical reality. Subsequently, scientific research was established as an essential social institution, and formal training and educational research centers at the university level began (LeVine 1984). This educational progress spread throughout Europe, where artisans, technicians, and craftsmen, who were the first genuine practitioners of modern research, were highly valued by the merchant class. They sponsored limited researchers and founded many institutions such as the Royal Society and the Academy of Science in England and France.

Rapid scientific and technological progress characterized the eighteenth and nineteenth centuries. The interdependence of science and technology was evident in the great inventions of the Industrial Revolution. More typically Thomas Edison's electric light and other inventions were based on the work of Michael Faraday and Joseph Henry; Alexander Graham Bell, the inventor of the telephone in 1876, based his work on that of Hermann Helmholtz; and Guglielmo Marconi, the inventor of radiography, on that of Heinrich Hertz and James Maxwell.

The modern concept of science and technology blossomed from the eighteenth century to the present, from Henri de Saint-Simon to Auguste Comte, Max Weber, and Karl Mannheim. Saint-Simon (1760-1825) envisioned an advanced industrial society of planners, engineers, scientists, and industrialists who would use technical knowledge to solve social problems. Mannheim, in opposition to his contemporaries like Weber, envisioned the fusion of knowledge and power in a classless elite who would apply technical knowledge to social planning (Boguslaw 1965). Mannheim reflected Karl Marx's belief that technology would end material scarcity as well as political conflict (Cole et al. 1983; Gunnel 1982). This is consistent with the widely accepted idea that technology leads to the end of ideology (Bell 1967). Technology would lead society to either utopia (B. F. Skinner, Howell, Edward Bellamy) or dystopia (George Orwell, Kurt Vonnegut, Aldous Huxley).

Yet, by the early twentieth century, the term "technology" was coming into general use and embraced a growing range of means, processes, and ideas in addition to tools and machines (Winner 1977). By the 1950s, there was a rising concern about the blurring line between scientific inquiry and technological activity. However, until quite recently, science has remained largely divorced from technology, each pursuing its separate path and maintaining its separate identity. "Pure" science is presumably concerned only with discovery of truth—the truth that is subject to observational and objective verification—and with the ordering and generalizing of mere facts into principles and laws of relationship sequence. Thus, while scientists are normally not concerned with utility, technologists have almost no other reason for their activities (Moore 1972). Whatever the intentions of those who formulate scientific principles, much of science nevertheless turns out to be practical, or to have practical applications. Some principles are even discovered and others amended in practice without preset intentions of the technologist.

Most scholars define technology, therefore, as the practical knowledge that relates ends to means. It is the organization of knowledge for the achievement of practical purposes (Mesthene 1970). Few scholars, however, use inclusive definitions. Ellul (1980), for instance, defines technology as social activity that is only prized in helping achieve something else. In this study, technology is defined as the means or activity by which people can apply discoveries, explorations, and inventions to natural science, thus fulfilling needs, satisfying desires for human development, and seeking to change and manipulate the environment.

About the middle of this century, theological thinkers and philosophers began to thematize technology. *The Technological Society* by Jacques Ellul and Herbert Marcuse's *One-dimensional Man* have launched the study of the materiality of technology, emphasizing its ultimate threat to the human spirit as if it already had become an uncontrollable force. Materiality, in the religious context, is often considered "symbolic" in function, the expression of an immaterial spirit. Philosophically, technology is "applied" theory dependent on "science which rises from pure thought." One essential and invariant dimension of technology is the extension of bodily skills, and its potential and actual amplification power. Technology provides higher speed (as time and distance factors) of human activity and accuracy of production (efficiency factor) (Ihde 1986).

This dominant understanding retains the view that technology extends science, that science "applies" technology. Yet Martin Heidegger argues that technology is ontologically prior to science and that science, far from being the origin of technology, is its necessary tool. Technology "sees" nature, takes it in a certain way, and "enframes" it. For this reason, technology precedes science. In this inversion of the usual interpretation, the very purity of theory functions as the tool of the metaphysics of "resources." Thus, both science and technology are embedded in a particular cultural trajectory. Neither is neutral, and both are part of an earlier metaphysical position. Although such an interpretation seems counterintuitive and contradictory to the dominant view, it provides another perspective to understand technology and society (Ihde 1986).

This view may be termed the "hermeneutic" dimension of technics—a technics used interpretively in an analogue with social construction of meaning rather than as an extension of bodily skills. The interpretive dimension of technology does not narrowly project technology as a "physical" force limited to an implicit model of the body and its extensions encapsulated by social meaning. Computers, new information technologies, and other contemporary technics portray the hermeneutic dimension of technology more starkly even if that dimension has always existed.

Three examples validate the interpretive dimension of technology in its social context. The first comes from the study of the consequences of the adoption of steel axes by Yir Yoront, a tribe of Australian aborigines (Sharp in Rogers 1983, 388). Before the introduction of steel axes by missionaries, the stone ax was the main tool in everyday life. It represented a symbol of masculinity and respect for the elders who owned them. Men used to lend these tools to women and children, the main users. Social custom ruled the rituals and relationships for borrowing and obtaining them. Although the steel ax expanded the bodily skills and amplified the capabilities of the tribe members, its use was limited to the same traditional functions, leaving the new-found leisure time for sleep. The missionaries' disappointment in the aborigines' failure to use the "new technology" for more productive and efficient ends, in fact, highlights Yir Yoront's worldview, which, embedded in their culture, limits the use of the steel ax. This example illustrates the problems of technology transfer to other societies whose interpretation of such new abilities is difficult to change in the absence of wider social development.

The second example illustrates the emergence of new innovation in response to social demand. Since the last century, the Industrial Revolution speeded up a society's material processing system. When the rapid increase in bureaucratic control could not handle the increase in information and organization of production, distribution, and processing activities, a control crisis ensued. Innovations in information processing and communication technologies lagged behind those of energy and its application to manufacturing and transportation. Complicated operations run at such human pace were inefficiently affecting railroads and mail services in America. A control mechanism had to be invented to deal with huge volumes of data, manage specialized knowledge, and organize tasks and processes. The early attempts to use mechanical devices finally succeeded in the development of electronic technology to manipulate information. The first computer, ENIAC, was produced to answer the need to store, process, and analyze national census data in 1946. The huge increment in microprocessing and computing technology is not a new force; it is merely the most recent installment in the continuing development of the "Control Revolution" (Beniger 1986).

The third example from the current debate on energy emphasizes the interpretive dimension of technology. The oil crisis in the early 1970s obligated changes in automobile technology to economize fuel consumption and produce smaller, more efficient models. Political conflict and rising economic power in the Middle East have influenced the use of prevailing technology in production processes. Despite their potential as a powerful and low-cost energy resource, nuclear power plants have been limited in their use to generate electric energy by environmental concerns. Local politics and social issues, then, have forced restricted application of the material dimension of technology.

By focusing on the materiality of technology, the problems of technics are often addressed too late, when technologies are already uncontrollable. A phenomenological hermeneutics of technology is required to explore both possibilities and limitations of technology. Society and technology are so closely intertwined that to examine one is to examine the other. In fact, technology is primarily social information.

It is important to emphasize this dialectical relationship between society and technology. Technology shapes the skills and abilities of labor and, therefore, establishes distinctive divisions of labor through its development. Technology also provides new opportunities and potential for social development. In turn, society has control over technology and manipulates it according to its needs and desires. Society dictates technology by interpretation and its construction of meaning.

In the next chapter, we will define a threefold scheme of current conditions along with escalating impact on society applying phenomenological hermeneutics of technology. The introduction of new information technologies and the social transformation toward a services- and information-based economy will be analyzed.

NOTES

1. Public transport ensured the integration of different zones and activities in the city, distributing the internal flow according to a bearable time/space relationship along their routes (Alonso 1964; Evans 1973).

2. The telephone launched the first two-way communication across distance, permitting further suburbanization and urban sprawl (Pool 1977).

3. The private car permitted home construction in remote areas devoid of public transportation. When viewed from the air, the spaces between the fingers of the starfish created by public transit lines are filled (Kling 1976; Adams 1970).

4. This trend remained the status quo for thousands of years, from ancient civilization through the Middle Ages, and governed further development in human activities, technology and division of labor. Yet, the limited commerce and the scanty communication among cities and the narrow needs of most of the population discouraged a higher division of labor.

5. The Fordism Model created a demand for new craft and intermediate-level skills while the average skill level of the work force remains steady or declines slowly. In the secondary sector firms, the great majority of the workers either have no skills or informally acquire capacities that are taken for granted (a young woman's ability to sew). They also include a few broadly skilled craftsmen who install, maintain, and supervise the operation of capital equipment (Sabel 1982).

6. In the early 1970s when shipyards in Brazil, Korea, and Turkey were adopting the new techniques and paid workers much lower wages, Sweden retreated from shipbuilding, illustrating the danger of traditional industrial production to developed countries. At present, Third World countries are building more heavy and light industries that were for a long time only in the hands of developed countries (Naisbitt 1982). This shift demonstrates the importance of a cheaper labor force, and more important, the Third World countries' ability to imitate and accept new innovations (Dos Santos 1970; Amin 1976; Frank 1980; Chilcote 1981). Furthermore, the emergence of international political power of recently independent nations demands a reformation of the economic order toward "fair" redistribution of world resources. This movement was initially proposed when seventy-seven members of the United Nations (the Group of 77) called for a New International Economic Order (NIEO) (Singh 1977; Kerr 1983).

7. Nevertheless, a certain element of modern science seems no less infused with the Cartesian character as it is with the ideals of Bacon (LeVine 1984). While both philosophers shared the insight that the possession of knowledge can be a powerful force, they were thinking of two different kinds of knowledge. For Bacon, knowledge was gained through experimentation. For René Descartes, knowledge was gained through mental awareness and comprehension in conceptualizing scientific inquiry, based on the deductive method to emphasize the role of the theoretical before the experimentation (Haberer 1969).

3

The Emergence of the Information Society

About thirty years ago, social scientists started to study social and economic development in Western countries, emphasizing the transitory nature of these changes. Colin Clark (1941) analytically divided any economy into three main components: primary sector—agriculture, secondary sector—manufacturing and industry, and tertiary sector—services. Any economy is a mixture in different proportions of each. He argued that as a nation becomes industrialized, a large proportion of the labor force enters manufacturing. As national income rises, because of sectoral differences in productivity, the demand for services and information rises. Several European theoreticians, such as Radovan Richta (1967), Serge Mallet (1963), and André Gorz (1968) have emphasized the decisive role of science and technology in transforming industrial structure in society. Brzezinski (1970), Ellul (1967), Galbraith (1967), and Lewis (1973) have developed theories that affirm the fusion of science and technology with the advanced working class.

Daniel Bell (1973) and Alain Touraine (1971) realized that industrial society no longer exists in developed countries. To Bell, a postindustrial society is defined by the expansion of an economy of services and the centrality of theoretical knowledge with a dominant class of professionals, engineers, technicians, and scientists. Touraine speaks of a "programmed society" defined by the emergence of new bureaucratic and professional social classes, by the new trend of business based on knowledge and organization, and by spare-time activities. On the other hand, McLuhan (1964) exposed another development of modern society. He argues that the appearance of new mass media in modern society transforms not only the social fabric, but also the individual's behavior and preference in a global village, which is apparent in economic interdependency and the international division of labor. The "transborder data flows" and culture exports influence every individual in work, entertainment, and social values. This is accomplished less by the sheer multiplication of information than by the way information is conveyed.

These concepts, despite their differences, indicate that a rapid socioeconomic transformation process is under way. This process constitutes what is conventionally called the "information society" whose characteristics are different from earlier agricultural and industrial societies. An information society is a nation in which a majority of the labor force is composed of information workers and in which the use and application of information is the most productive element in its economy (Porat 1978). Table 3.1 summarizes a comparison of the agricultural, industrial, and information societies and their developmental characteristics. Eventually, the three "societies" coexist simultaneously in any society.

By 1954 the United States was the first country to become an information society (Machlup 1962; Rogers 1984). In 1980, only 3 percent of the United States labor force were agricultural workers, with 76 percent in services and information activities (Porat 1978).[1] David Birch more recently found that over 80 percent of all newly created jobs are in information and service sectors (Naisbitt 1982). Most Western European countries, Canada, and Japan are following the same trend toward information societies.[2] In fact, Japan has become an information society or *johoka shakai* since 1966 (Ito 1981).

The information society encompasses several changes in socioeconomic development: (1) a change from goods to services— rapidly increasing the human-oriented service sector such as professional, technical, educational, health, and fast-food industries;

(2) a change in the character of work—work is primarily a "game" among persons in their daily experience (professionals and clients, salesmen and customers); (3) a change toward the growth of the knowledge class—by 1975 more than 25 percent of the labor force in the United States were in the technical and professional class; (4) a technological change toward high-tech industry, whose main products are small devices and affordable machines that generate, manipulate, and transmit information, such as semiconductors and microelectronics; and (5) a change in the spread of new information technologies and the development of telecommunications for remote services and activities with the explosive growth of computers.

SOCIOECONOMIC MODEL OF THE
INFORMATION SOCIETY

Technology always influences ways societies choose to interact in economic activity, which could be explained in a production-consumption model. The following model responds to the current social transformation toward information society (figure 3.1). This model explains the dialectical relationship of two factors. The first is changes in proportions and characteristics of the two main production sectors—information and industry. This model classifies industrial production into traditional and high-tech industries, each with distinct demands for skilled labor, organization behavior, and location decisions. The information sector is divided into home-based services and information industries according to their demand for information and knowledge. The second factor is the diffusion of hundreds of innovations and information applications that have emerged exponentially in the past few years. They are categorized into three subsectors: information services and software, communication channels, and infrastructure and hardware.

The integration of production sectors, which produce information devices, and the diffusion of new information technologies, which promotes high-tech industries and information sectors, produce fundamental changes in socioeconomic activities. Individuals who are engaged in new conditions of production and

Table 3.1
Evolution of Societies: A Comparison of Agricultural, Industrial, and Information Societies

CHARACTERISTIC	AGRICULTURAL	INDUSTRIAL	INFORMATION
Beginning of Society	8,000 B.C.	17th Century	1950s
Country of Origin	Egypt	England	U.S.A.
Basic Technology	Manual Labor	Steam Engine	Semiconductor
Technological Advancement	Agricultural Tools	Energy	Information
Role of Technology	Extraction	Fabrication	Process
Technological Focus	Irrigation	Mechanization & Standardization	Processing
Main Product	Food	Commodities	Knowledge
Main Labor Force	Farmers	Factory Workers	Information Workers
Avarage Skills (Worker)	Increase	Decrease	Increase

28

Division of Labor (Skills)	Simple (Multiple Tasks)	Highly Specialized (Routine)	Very High (Information Rich/Poor)
Division of Labor (Geographically)	City	Regional	International
Social Institution	Farm	Steel Mills / Auto Factories	R.&D. Centers / Universities
City Function	Authority	Manufacturing	Services
Polis (Major trend)	Anthropo	Megalo	Tele
Urbanization Trend	Gradual	Exponential	Diffused/Reversal
City Pattern	Human Network	Transportation	Multinodal
Main Mode of Movement	Pedestrian	Vehicular	And Telecommuting
Land Uses	Mixed (Res. & Comm.)	Segregated	Mixed (Res. & Work)
Type of Services	Daily (Localized)	Specialized (Economy of Scale)	Customized (Delocalized)
Marketplace	Agora/ Forum	CBD/Mall	Electronic Network
City Problems	Crowdedness	Slums/Traffic/Pollution	Isolation/Unemployment

Figure 3.1
Socioeconomic Model of Information Society and Its Impact on City Form

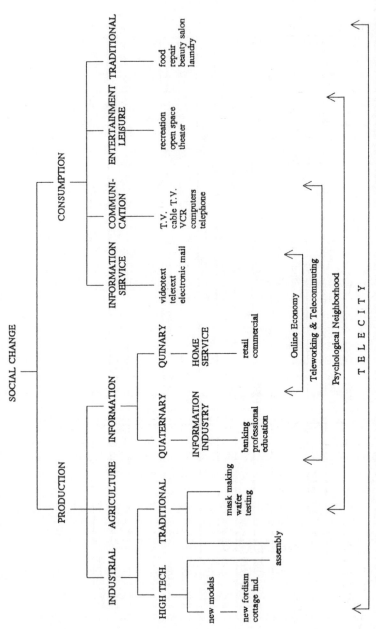

divisions of labor, and, at the same time, are consumers of new information and communication machines, are influenced in their daily working activities. New economic activities have emerged to benefit from the potential of information technologies, and new ways of consumption and production are underway. This socioeconomic model of information society is presented in the following.

FIRST: PRODUCTION

New information technologies are strategic for generating, processing, and transmitting data, information, and knowledge (Bell 1973). An information sector is based on codification and assimilation of knowledge (Gershuny 1978), and the crucial power variable is the control of information.

The information sector of production consists of three subsectors. First, tertiary activity includes transportation and utilities. Second, knowledge-based activity (quaternary) includes trade, finance, insurance, banking, and real estate. Third, information services (quinary) take in health, education, research, government, and recreation activities (Bell 1973, table I.I). The information sector gain of labor has absorbed (in absolute numbers) the surplus in agricultural workers, while the percentage of industrial workers in the labor force has remained almost steady.

Information is a unique economic commodity. It lacks a physical existence of its own except through the organization and movement of extraneous matter and energy such as paper and ink, computers and monitors, and electrical power and television. It can be sold just as often as demand allows without ever being consumed. Therefore, it can easily transfer and exchange.[3]

In both traditional and high-tech industries, current conditions have altered production activities. Industrial production has displaced most large firms of traditional industries in the mass market for standardized goods with more specialized, high-quality products. Sabel (1982) argues that specialization often demands collaboration between designer and skilled producers to make a variety of goods with general-purpose machinery. On these bases, two models emerged: the Neo-Fordism model of production and the high-tech cottage industry.

The Neo-Fordism model depends on enlarging the range of mass production goods within limits compatible with flexible automated systems likely to be available in the near future. Ideally, an industry would like to meet the demands of different markets by designing a range of products composed of a limited set of modules in various combinations and producing them using the new techniques. For example, various General Motors models are built on a single chassis and equipped with a variety of prestigious trim.

The second production model, high-tech cottage industry, is developed in small towns near Bologna, Italy. It originated in small firms of only five to fifty highly skilled workers where difference between supervisor and employee is barely distinguishable. The workers remain closer to the artisan tradition where they can adjust quickly according to the circumstances. Each product is the most advanced, numerically controlled item of its type—sophisticated, flexible, and distinctive enough to capture world markets. They export precision machine tools to the United States, Japan, and the rest of Europe.

These two new production models require highly skilled labor who can combine conception and execution. Those who perform the work and those who determine the nature and method of production to meet changing demands are one and the same. Production increasingly depends on innovations in flexible automation, which can be quickly reprogrammed to perform various operations, such as robots, to replace both the specialized machinery and unskilled laborers.

Another branch of industrial production is high-tech industries. They demonstrate a technological change in the production process and organizational structure. They are characterized by their rapid rate of change in underlying technology, a higher ratio of R&D expenditures to sales (about 1:10), and worldwide competition (Rogers and Valente 1988). Thus, high-tech is "high" not only because its technology is complicated or sophisticated, but also because its rate of change is high.[4] The main production categories are micro-electronics, telecommunications and information systems, automation, genetic engineering, and advanced technological materials (Castells 1984). The industrial outcome is process-oriented rather than product-oriented. Communication, for example, is a transmission vehicle to organize a message; it is not the message (which is information product). Integrated circuits are basically used for control devices or central processing units to be used, in turn, to produce or perform other tasks. Their main purpose is processing, generating, or transmitting information such as telecommunications, software, and computers.

Take as an example semiconductors, the basic product of the electronics industry, which exhibit all the characteristics of high-tech production. They are science-based industry depending entirely on new conditions of knowledge, information, scientific personnel, and technical labor. The process of production is composed of four different phases that can be spatially separated (even internationally) to benefit from distinct skilled labor requirements. These phases are: (1) design and mask making, which is engineering the circuit that goes into the chip and reducing it through lithography. This phase requires highly specialized, research-trained personnel; (2) wafer fabrication, where the circuit is made into wafers that undergo a series of complex operations before being cut into individual chips. This phase requires highly skilled workers and quality control supervision; (3) assembly, where the chips are gathered to form integrated circuits, a routine, labor-intensive operation; and (4) testing, which is a capital-intensive, widely automated process. These phases of production can be clustered in two main divisions of labor: highly skilled labor for mask making, wafer fabrication, and testing; and low-skilled labor for the assembly process (Saxenian 1984).

The production process of high-tech industries has major locational implications. The current trend of production decentralization attempts to take advantage of locational factors (cheaper real estate, accessibility, weather) while core industries remain centralized in main metropolitan areas to control planning, finance, marketing, and more importantly innovation with links to R&D centers. This dispersed pattern is evident in the United States and Europe and has exhibited footloose features, such as the Silicon Valley in Northern California (Rogers and Larsen 1984; Miller and Cote 1985), Route 128 in Boston (Saxenian 1985), and Austin, Texas (Farely and Glickman 1986; Gibson and

Rogers 1988). Many recent studies have investigated the tendency of some high-tech industries to cluster with rapid urban sprawl (Castells 1985; Markusen et al. 1986, Rogers 1988). The accompanying economic growth of these places has encouraged many local authorities to induce high-tech growth poles. Notions such as "technopolis" are emerging.

The "technopolis" is capturing attention for its potential for economic growth (Simlor et al. 1988). It is a new urban form where the main economic activity is high-tech industries and related services. It is usually located according to interstitial conditions of collaboration of R&D activities among private industry, research universities, and government agencies. The presence of venture capital and entrepreneurial spin-off firms contributes to settlement in a pleasant and accessible location. The application of this concept is attracting a growing audience.

The current conditions of production—new models of industrial production and the emergence of high-tech industries—also have a dramatic impact on restructuring the division of labor. The labor market tends to have an increasingly large amount of highly skilled labor, while the need for semi- and unskilled labor is diminishing. The gap between levels of skill will increase. The need for industrial, unskilled cheap wage labor in certain phases of high-tech based industries (assembly) is emerging along with the production of traditional, less profitable products and commodities to form a new trend of shifting toward the world labor market, and consequently, a new international division of labor among countries for a single good. This configuration will result in determining the way members of society engage in everyday activity of production and consumption.

SECOND: DIFFUSION OF NEW INFORMATION TECHNOLOGIES

The consumption of information and high-tech products has resulted in diffusion of new information technologies to various groups and social institutions that realize their advantages and potentials. New information technologies are mostly friendly innovations and, therefore, rapidly diffused but not easily noticed. The habitual nature of these rapidly diffused innovations makes them a vital part of our daily lives. Since 1876, the diffusion of the telephone service launched the first two-way personal communication, which quickly became the dominant means of communicating among people around the globe. Telephones, color television, and VCRs are now virtual necessities for the majority of American households. Personal computers and satellite communications are following the same trend.

By all means, we are experiencing a technological revolution, informational in nature. This revolution started with the first catalyst (*Sputnik* satellite) in 1957, initiating an era of global satellite communication (Naisbitt 1982). It was followed by the integration of computers and telecommunications, which form the core product of technological change. It depends on the manufacturing of integrated circuits and semiconductor chips because of their increasing information power. Now new information technologies are able to process, transmit, and interconnect all information (images, texts, and voice) produced in one area instantly to remote destinations.[5] The notions of "wired city" (Webber 1973), "global village" (McLuhan 1964), and "electronic cottage" (Toffler 1980) have recently become realities due to new technology, which has introduced advanced information systems and communication networks to our societies.

Obviously, a single technical feat, no matter how much attention is showered upon it, does not in itself constitute a complete technological transformation. Indeed, one of the characteristics of a true technological revolution is the "swarm" effect—a great many innovations taking place almost simultaneously. Their integration creates a synergistic and explosive impact upon the production of goods and services. But technology does not occur in a vacuum; it takes place in its social context. Social acceptance and interpretation and their diffusion in political, economic, and social institutions make a revolution within society.

Furthermore, these systems accelerate diffusion of innovation to remote areas, illustrating the three fundamental dimensions of technology: speed, which alters time and distance; routine and accurate processes, a core materialistic dimension; and the interpretive dimension of understanding and transmission of information and knowledge.

Characteristics of New Information Technologies

New information technologies are differentiated from the previous increments of technological development by featuring low unit costs, high speed, and versatile information processing (Wad 1982). First, they tend to be *interactive:* users deal directly with each other through two-way telecommunication systems, which makes communications much like interpersonal interactions. This interactivity is expected to be more accurate, effective, and satisfying to the participant in a communication process. Second, they are *individualized* (de-massified)—the control of the communication system is with the user. Messages can be designed for a particular member of society to satisfy individual need. Third, they are *asynchronous:* they have the capability to receive a message whenever it is convenient for the individual user rather than the sender, a time shifting in interaction (Rogers 1985). Fourth, they tend to be *customized.* It is possible to provide specialized services to certain groups. And finally, they offer *proximity* of information to reach more people regardless of distance.

The constant reduction of interactive communications costs will enhance the use of new information technologies. Since the technology deployed to connect any two points on earth is almost the same regardless of their relative geographic distance, the actual cost of local communication in the Los Angeles metropolitan area, for instance, will be almost the same as similar communication between Los Angeles and New York, further decreasing the virtual distance.

On the other hand, new information technologies display a unique characteristic. They embody "amplification-reduction" quality (Ihde 1986), which extends, for instance, verbal reach throughout the world by telephone network, but also perceptually reduces sensory experience. Human experience is reduced to a mono-sensory dimension of hearing (without the full sensation in action). Distance is reduced to nearness, but that remains partially distorted by machine mediation. Technological gains of great scope simultaneously lose partial perception of the real world.

THE IMPACT OF NEW INFORMATION
TECHNOLOGIES ON CITIES

The consequences of the rapid change in new information technologies on cities could be distinctively traced in three major integrated levels of invention.

Telecommunication Infrastructure and Hardware

This subsector includes the basic hardware components of telecommunication systems, such as satellites, cables, the application
of microwaves, fiber optics, and lasers to increase capacities for
the transmission of information. Cable receivers, television stations, mainframe computers, and transmitters are some elements
of the subsector.

Three principal trends characterize electronic hardware today:
reduction in cost, improvement in reliability, and increase in
packing density (the number of components in single volume).
Each of these characteristics of technology has been changing by
approximately one hundred per decade since 1960. Studies by
The Future Group indicate that these trends can continue for at
least another two decades (Guile 1985).

A variety of telecommunications systems is used at the local or
regional level, such as microwaves, coaxial cables, fiber optics,
and cellular mobile radio. The cellular radio technology makes it
potentially feasible for every car or remote place to have a communication line. This mobile phone capability is now spreading
rapidly to become independent from the limits and costs of cable
networks.

The direct impact of this level of invention is limited to city
form. Most of the infrastructure is embedded underground, or
uses previous utility lines (telephone network, rail tracks) or even
facilities that are invisible to city inhabitants (microwaves, elec-
tromagnetic transmission).

A recent development in telecommunications infrastructure,
the "teleport," is the most obvious physical form of advancement
in communication technology, receiving and transmitting infor-

mation via satellites that bypass expensive national communication networks. Teleport consists of a large field of hundreds of different size dish receivers and a fiber optic cable network. Similar in application to the old-fashioned railroad station or the modern airport, teleport is the harbinger of a new type of public service.

Many teleport projects are now operating. New York teleport demonstrates new cooperation between private firms (Merrill Lynch) and public authorities (JFK Airport and the City of New York) to sponsor construction of the first teleport in Staten Island. Recent study (Moss 1986) showed that twenty new teleport projects followed in twelve different states; eleven of these facilities are operational, and the rest are planned.

Communication Channels

This subsector is centered on a combination of computers and telecommunications in interactive information networks: broadcasting channels of radio, FM stations, television stations, cable television, VCRs, and home computers. The personal computer, for instance, has paved the way for applications in many areas of information processing, while the mass production of VCRs has allowed "time shifting": viewers can watch their favorite television programs when they wish. Cable television has made the 1970s notion of the "wired city" a reality. In 1982 over 65 percent of American households were connected to cable television service (Williams 1982). Both VCRs and cable television with hundreds of channels have radically influenced the entertainment industries by moving the site of the activity into homes from specialized public theaters.

Although the personal computer manifests typical new information technologies, it is largely considered a new communication channel due to its interactive capability. By 1985, personal computers had diffused to more than 15 percent of United States households, with many possessing more than one machine (Rogers 1985). As technological development advances, we will become surrounded by computers, from large ones handling business tasks to microcomputers in our cars, appliances, toys, games, entertainment centers, and potentially everywhere.

The many uses for telecommunications in our daily lives can be summed up as "instrumental" and "intrinsic." Among instrumental uses are emergencies, news, and direct information. Among the intrinsic uses are the social contacts they facilitate between friends, relatives, neighbors, and the world (Keller in Pool 1977).

Information Services and Software

Software consists of coded instructions that enable individuals to use information technology. This subsector includes data, information, programs, and services that are stored and transformed by information systems. Software is vital not only to the operation of information systems, but also to their ability to interlink with each other, with data bases, and with people. The demand for software is skyrocketing—tailoring systems to customer needs, making them more reliable, and achieving user simplicity (Mayo 1985). Additionally, software provides a variety of information services to individuals and firms as well, which change the time and distance dimensions in the supplier-user relationship. In contrast to the movement of conventional services or goods through conventional infrastructure transportation networks, information services are transmitted to customers through cable telephone lines or through broadcasting. Videotext, teletext, and telemarketing are typical applications of telecommunications sector.[6] Answering service and voice mail are more recent personalized services within a wider range of direct dialing, teleconferencing, and announcement.

The expanded use of automated teller machines (ATMs) adds the convenience of twenty-four-hour banking. Banks have encouraged the implementation of ATMs to reduce transaction costs and provide extended services to their customers. ATMs have multiplied and are widely accepted by customers. It seems to many banking analysts that the wider distribution of ATMs suggests a leading edge and is becoming a competitor turf for banks. Many retail establishments install ATMs on their premises to provide means for their customers to obtain ready cash. "Cash points" have become more popular to exploit the versatility of ATMs to connect customers to their various banks, analogous to the way telephone networks are operated by different companies. This feature will ensure higher usage of these machines. Currently, ATMs account for approximately one-half of all regular banking transactions (Gordon 1985).

The proliferation of software products and computer programs into many areas from organizations to public domain highlights the manipulation and availability of channels to diversify information and messages. Office automation, for example, transformed work processes and will alter organizational structure.

However, software is currently the bottleneck in information technology. While its development is difficult and costly, productivity is improving thanks to computer aids for software design, which eventually should lead to automatic generation of application programs. Soon a wide spectrum of user-friendly software systems will be available, so that most users can buy functional applications to perform necessary tasks.

As we have shown, each of the three levels of information technology exhibits distinctive features. However, it seems that any application may involve all and have joint impacts on the city. It is most evident in altering ways and means of interpreting one's position in regard to economic activity of production (job) and consumption (shopping, entertainment, services). The economic activities of production and consumption are interlinked, in that each individual engages in both through taste and talents, which structure the socioeconomic conditions of society. The technological transformation of Western society promises technological impacts on the new development of the city.

EMERGENCE OF TELEACTIVITY

Teleactivity is socioeconomic activity based on interactive, individualized, and asynchronous telecommunication systems to connect persons, tasks, and information regardless of distance. In the last ten years the "inconvenience costs" of interaction among geographically separated points have declined consistently while the capacity for the exchange and use of information has increased dramatically. Travel time between pairs of points has been reduced significantly. New communication devices have had a powerful effect on the quality of life through the radically improved accessibility that has accompanied teleactivity.

Distinctive levels of teleactivities have emerged from (1) the interaction among new characteristics of information systems, and (2) the shift in the economic activities toward information. (See figure 3.1.) Among many levels, three are introduced in the following section: online economy, teleworking, and psychological neighborhood.

The Online Economy: Electronic Mall

An "online" economy has emerged from the integration of information services technology with the "home service economy." It consists of services (retail, entertainment, and information) sent directly to the customer in the convenience of the home. Telemarketing, telebanking, and teleshopping are reaching more households. The diversity made possible by transmission technologies (telephone lines, television broadcasting, cable television, and fiber optics) makes it easier to react with customized responses to the needs of various social groups.

Compu-Serve, Source, and Dialog are examples of this new level of teleactivities that allow interactive communication among points on the surface of the earth. To open a new facility is simply to add a new data base to the current electronic facility. By 1988, 2 million subscribers had been linked to these electronic outlets.

With this close interaction between business and home a basic level of teleactivity is flourishing. The development of the online economy is more likely to conform to the desires and predispositions of households than to determine them. However, businesses, since they are organized primarily for profit, are more adaptive to opportunities provided by technology than are individuals. Consequently, businesses are expected to exploit further the rich sources of information technologies to attract more customers.

The online economy changes the consumer-producer relationship. It can afford sizable discounts because it eliminates space requirements and inventory costs. Products arrive directly from the manufacturer while a printout of choices offers a quick way to compare products. The new "electronic mall" concept is being developed to offer the convenience of a shopping center at home with large variety and competitive products. Like other information services, it can significantly increase individual access to national upscale markets while reducing the cost of capturing and processing an order (Sigel 1983).

In the electronic mall, a huge commercial, retail, and service data base is hosted in a virtual network of videotext, teletext, and telemarketing. These information services have changed organizational firms and business by expanding the market and creating new boundaries for the business delivery system. Suppliers are motivated to participate in the new information systems by exposing their products and services to more customers because they can relax their own constraint of rents, large inventory of merchandise, and transportation cost.

On the other hand, customers will benefit from information services. They will be able to obtain consumer goods at lower prices whle easily comparing prices and product specifications. A buyer can display, retrieve, and print all of the needed information about products and delivery time in different stores. Users and buyers will have the advantage of higher levels of competition and be able to purchase the latest fashions or their airline ticket through their convenient home keyboard.

Teleworking and the Workplace

Teleworking became possible when the computer moved onto the worker's desk. It has become a reality through the integration among new channels of interactive communication and the change in the nature of office work based on information transmission. Teleworkers spend one or more days per week working at home using microcomputers—which may be connected to the workplace by telecommunciations—or remote terminals connected to the home office computer system. Telecommunication uses include voice communications, electronic messaging, document transmission, and interactive computer programming (Nilles 1984). As the infrastructure becomes widely accessible, substantial areas of production can transfer from centralized and specialized buildings back into the home; routine typing and record keeping are obvious candidates creating the "back office" phenomenon in residential areas (Cross and Raizman 1986).

Teleworking centers are designed to reduce the costs of business location, transportation, and time. Each involves a remote work center close to workers' homes. The general office environment differs from the traditional in that the members of individual work units or groups may be scattered among several different centers, each closer to the worker's residence. As a result, a better combination of face-to-face and telecommunication interaction can be achieved among the members of the work unit. Theoretically, the worker could live anywhere—in the mountains, near the beach, or in another city, unconstrained by the location of the employer.

Teleworking, instituted to improve employee working conditions, includes reduction of commuting time, provision of flexible working conditions, provision of time or space unavailable in the office environment, and convenient child care. It provides wide opportunities for women to work closer to home (Baran 1985; Madden 1981). On the other hand, employer benefits include the ability to recruit or retain workers whose skills are in strong demand, the geographical extension of the labor pool, and the expansion of part-time, single parent, and handicapped workers. The reduction of office space and equipment costs, and the flexibility of expanding to meet occasional work demands are possible advantages to the employer (Baer 1985; Dordick and Williams 1986).

Statistical evidence about American teleworkers is scarce. In 1986, approximately 200,000 to 250,000 employees were engaged in some sort of teleworking. However, it is estimated that the number will reach 18 million by 1995 (Peterson 1987).

Teleworking is starting to involve government agencies' facilitators as the community benefits of telecommuting are recognized. It reduces both construction costs for upgrading and maintaining transportation infrastructure and social costs of reducing congestion and air pollution (Southern California Association of Governments 1985).

The most active attempt to implement teleworking among U.S. agencies has been undertaken by the Southern California Association of Governments (SCAG) in response to the problem of a budget shortfall of $51 billion to maintain and rehabilitate transportation systems in this decade. In its search for the application of telecommunication technologies and implementation of teleworking policy, SCAG furnishes technical assistance to its 200 member governments and to interested corporations through its transportation and communications committee. In June 1986, SCAG mounted a pilot project involvng 15 of its 130 employees. One of their studies (1985) indicated that if only 12 percent of the labor force teleworks, congestion in the current transportation system will decrease by 32 percent.

Psychological Neighborhood: The Image

Any system that increases travel speed or reduces its cost is likely to encourage people to live farther away from their jobs or other places they visit frequently. Improvements in accessibility of activities encourage dispersion of both homes and activities. Telecommunication systems are speeding this process of decentralization for jobs and services. Thus, city centers are no longer favored over other places.

New information technologies, such as the telephone, draw neighbors and communities together by providing people with shared networks. Unlike mass communications, they may be described as "discretionary," allowing the user to select the service and the time to call (see Pierce in Pool 1977). In fact, the telephone is considered a basic device and essential part of our social communication. Its use becomes habitual rather than conscious. A common assumption in our everyday interaction relies on the "guaranteed" access to the telephone network.

The boundaries of one's social reality are no longer rooted in the contiguous space but in a kind of "symbolic proximity" that replaces the supportive nature of daily interactions with the potential of instant remote contact. As Dubos (1972) argues, an internalized "conceptual environment" is such a subjective construct that it conditions one's sense of socialization as surely as the built environment's tangible influence.

A "psychological neighborhood" would not be merely a mental

landscape beginning at the border of the actual neighborhood, but one that superimposed itself upon the immediate environs, drawing the individual into a home-based electronic web and out of the kind of street life that reduces isolation and makes a neighborhood a more supportive community (Wurtzel and Turner 1977).

A psychological neighborhood is created in every individual's image to connect places (or functions) in "virtual structures" depending on interactive communication with work, shopping, entertainment, and social relations. These seamless webs create a "self-social group" linked in a communication network independent of actual locations, with the time structure of interaction controlled by the parties. Some activities, of course, will cognitively separate these levels of linkages, each with comparable functions. These virtual communities of communication networks are based on households and individuals who engage in similar activities and interests, with their boundaries determined not so much by distance as by the capability of the electronic network and its new information technologies.

THE EMERGENCE OF THE TELECITY

The aggregation of teleactivities on the city scale foreshadows a major modification in the image of the city, its locational patterns, and the composition of its social and economic activities. Teleactivities are affecting future communities by transforming them from a basis of territoriality and proximity to "communities without propinquity" by breaking down their confinement. Many workers will live, act, work, entertain, and shop in the convenience of their homes regardless of their dispersed spatial pattern. They will watch television, buy from teleshopping using teletext or telemarketing, telecommute to their jobs, and socialize by telecommunications. In the near future people will live in telecities where working activity and leisure time will mingle.

Communication networks will link people, tasks, resources, and management into various configurations of both temporary and permanent organizations. They can be formed quickly, do their business, disperse, reform again, and so on—not physically, but in limitless "information space" (Nanus 1982). Business firms are likely to divide production, services, management, sales, and repair processes in wide spatial pattern among cities and regions.

The diversification of working processes can benefit from locational advantages of each space, with the link between manufacturing and commerce fragmented into smaller stages, and without simple organizational structure. Some cities will have a dominant business on a large regional domain as their built environments or geographical characteristics may suggest for specific services. Furthermore, cities may not be the only center of economic activity; they will face strong competition from rural areas. Ruralization can also be advanced by attracting footloose information services to locate part of their activities in rural provisions.

Because the marketplace will be located virtually in communication networks instead of physically in stores and warehouses, information services can connect the needs and resources of users to the capabilities and services of producers and facilitate these transactions. Customers can contact a sales assistant in any city; their checks would be forwarded to another city; the product is manufactured in a third place (or abroad); and the warehouse is not necessarily in any of these places. Thus, producers and consumers deal with each other in teleplaces—telecities.

Since people still need physical mobility in their interaction and social life, the new spatial structure of the city of the future is generated by the overlay of transportation and communication networks on a multinodal, nonlocational system. The resulting major changes in city function and structure produce the "telecity," where remote services, facilities, and work dominate city life. Telecity accommodates teleworkers and provides information services to both its inhabitants and other customers based on telecommunication networks. Without a critical mass in the city of the future, the telecity cannot exist. Interactive networks demand the engagement of a sufficient number of points to assure the diffusion of tele-activities, otherwise teleactivities would be imputed.

The telecity concept is a place of endless psychological neighborhoods—probably one for each inhabitant's cognitive map. The two concepts should not be confused. The psychological neighborhood is a cognitive scheme created in the individual mind to link his own activities interactively in nonlocational relationships. Telecity, on the other hand, is a place where a critical mass of individuals shares access to multilevel teleactivities. Telecity provides its inhabitants with the means for new information technologies whose psychological neighborhoods may overlap. The psychological neighborhood concept is individually based, while the telecity concept is collectively based. Both exhibit different physical dimensions—the psychological neighborhood is placeless, yet telecity spatially exists and is virtually connected to the whole world.

The telecity is the concentration of individuals, households, firms, and public agencies who interactively communicate and interconnect via remote services and facilities, and work in a wide geographical area. Los Angeles can be considered to be at the first stage of a telecity with its thirty-five distributed subcenters. Telecommunication appears to have strategic importance to arrange any kind of social and economic activity in its widely expanded landscape.

The next chapter examines the propositions of the emergence of multilevel teleactivities and their aggregation to create telecity. Applying an appropriate research design will validate these assumptions.

NOTES

1. Since the agricultural sector's share in the labor force and national product is limited in modern society, it does not heavily influence the current transformation process, nor does it occupy a central part in technological change.

2. The information society does not displace the industrial society, but the new developments overlay the previous social characteristics. Indeed the introduction of new technologies does not always mean the complete demise of older technologies (Kranzberg 1985).

3. The shift toward information-based activities is accompanied by social problems such as unemployment, invasions of privacy, information inequality, and high segregation in division of labor based solely on skills (Salvagio 1983). Workers, particularly the middle-aged, have to acquire new abilities and skills to be able to use new industrial machines or automated office equipment (Rogers 1984).

4. Definitions of high-technology sectors can be either more or less restrictive or inclusive, based on as many as eighteen variables. The U.S. Bureau of Labor Statistics identifies 36 out of 977 industries as high-tech based mainly on the employment rate of R&D and technical employment to the U.S. average (2:1). It helps to standardize the definition to some degree (Malecki 1984).

5. New information technologies are the hardware equipment, organizational structures, and social values through which individuals collect, process, and exchange information.

6. Videotext is an interactive information service that allows individuals to request frames of information from a central computer via telephone line or cable television for viewing on a video display screen (usually a home television receiver or a computer monitor). Videotext can provide any user with an infinite number of pages of information, data, or shopping items (Sigel 1983). Teletext allows individuals, using a decoder, to select a page number from about 100-400 frames of information for viewing on home television screens. It is transmitted in the "vertical blanking intervals" of the conventional television broadcast signal (Rogers 1985).

4

An Application
of Futures Research

The study of the social impact of technology belongs to a class of problems in the social sciences that requires a more complex logic than that of simple causality (direct relationship among few variables and their explicit sequences). Dual effects are one reason for the paucity of the literature on its impact. Moreover, the rapid advances of information technology make any study of its consequences much more difficult to pin down. Therefore, a study of the impact of new information technologies should account for the fast-paced change by addressing future changes rather than studying only the present moment.

The future lies in the domain of goals, and its plasticity makes it more important to study and more difficult to predict (Cornish 1977). Since the future is seldom a mere temporal continuation of past, it is likely to be significantly different from the present.

The study of the future implies the use of forecasting techniques. Forecasting applies available information to predict consequences of present policies and to propose actions to achieve desired goals. Forecasting, however, is not mere prediction; it needs to account for contextual situations, and uses informed judgments about events to draw a wide range of possible consequences.[1] As such, many forecasting methods qualify as tools for planning public policymaking. Yet, the field of planning seldom devotes enough attention to forecasts (Wachs 1985).[2]

In a broad sense, planning represents social attempts to order the environment to achieve certain goals.[3] It is concerned not with just the rational allocation of resources but, more important, the selection of goals and values to be achieved (Weaver in Duhl 1963). Planning is decisions about which goals should be pursued and which actions should be taken. It projects a future.[4] For that, planning is concerned with dynamic forecasting—the process by which a decision maker can identify the extent of influencing events in the future as a function of present resources. Consequently, dynamic forecasting requires innovative research methods that deal with complexity and prospective aspects of the problem to yield reliable and consistent conclusions.

Futures research methods are appropriate techniques for social forecasting. Their fundamental assumption postulates that society is not predestined or otherwise constrained to a particular long-run end state. Their procedures are based on two concepts: *robustness* and *cybernetics*. Robustness works with fundamental causes of change as the basis for designing new strategic options consistent with anticipated future environments (Nanus 1982). A robust concept can withstand large environmental changes. It provides effective performance under all likely future environments to enable flexible adjustment to these changes. Cybernetics is based on the perception that a single present situation will induce a set of alternative futures via a cybernetic process, and the future should only be viewed within a wide range of expectations. Futures research methods require more than observation; they require judgmental interpretation to relate past to future to prepare for action.

Futures studies can be characterized by the general ambition to support decision making by supplying relevant information for a long-range perspective (Boucher 1977, 6-9). The function of futures research is to extend the range of public vision to encompass new alternative futures as well as reduce the uncertainty of events. Futures research methodologies have the ability to prepare sufficient information with a set of probabilities into the planning process. They do not forecast the "future" but generate possible alternative "futures" (King 1975).

The Delphi method, QUEST (Quick Environmental Scanning Technique), computer-based simulation techniques such as

INTERAX (Interactive Cross-Impact Analysis), and scenario generating are some techniques developed to deal with specific futures research problems. Each is applied to a variety of situations ranging from forming precepts of possible futures to the study of probable alternatives. The usefulness and viability of any methods depend crucially on the organizational and policy-making framework in which any particular project is embedded as well as on the futures study's objectives (Schwarz et al. 1982).

The Delphi method, pioneered by Olaf Helmer and his associates at the Rand Corporation, is a widely used polling technique that systematically and collectively solicits expert subjective opinions in quantified form. At the same time, it maintains the heterogeneity of the participants to assure validity of the results and avoid the dominance of aggregating results by quantity. While some individual responses may be more informative and accurate, the aggregation process assimilates this expertise. Each response, then, should also be individually considered in assessing the scope of the exercise. This method, in fact, systemizes and rationalizes the procedure of making informed guesses.

The use of the Delphi method in planning is conventionally limited to its cybernetic feature designed to reach a consensus on conflicting issues, to choose from a set of policy alternatives, or to distinguish crucial differences among expert groups. Actually, the technique was developed to deal with various research questions: technology assessment, alternative solutions to complicated problems, and structural changes in future events.

In this research, I adopted the Delphi method to verify the conceptual analysis of the effects of teleactivities on social transformation. This application of the Delphi method is novel. I do not use it to forecast procedure, generate hypotheses, or evoke implications about the future. Instead, this method is used to validate concepts of emerging levels of the teleactivities creating telecity and exposing their consequences.

My use of this method depends on neither Lockean nor Leibnizian philosophy, as it is neither built on empirical (inductive) representations of the problem nor theoretical (deductive) derivations. This method relies on Kantian philosophy, emphasizing the synthetic system of matching theory to data. Since future events are not empirically explicit, this method makes explicit the strong interaction between the model (telecity) and the collected data (Mitroff and Turoff 1975).[5]

This Dynamic Design Process Delphi (DDPD), a version of the "policy" Delphi, is based on the premise that decision makers are not interested so much in having a group generate decisions but rather, in having an informed group validate the bases of decision to be taken, revise the effectiveness of the design approach to formulate the required policy, and present all options and supporting evidence for consideration. In this way, the DDPD method operates as precursor to the decision-making activity in a dynamic environment (Turoff, 1975).

In short, the purposes of this exercise are to: (1) validate concepts and consequences observed and critically analyzed prior to the exercise by a wide range of experts—their aggregated judgments assuring confidence in these concepts and events without diluting the importance of any individual response; (2) bring to the planning process a wide scope of possible expectations within which desired goals and operational alternatives can be designed; and (3) develop a theoretical model to explore planning options for understanding complex change in city form. This method is a generic concept of using and organizing knowledge and of presenting the final results.

RESEARCH DESIGN

The initial goal of the research design was to recruit between thirty and forty experts in physical planning, urban analysis, and the social impact of technology, who are familiar with both technology and urban form. This criterion was the basis for selecting potential experts and evaluating their final participation. I selected a list of 265 experts from two large nationwide mailing lists: those of the School of Urban and Regional Planning and the Center for Telecommunications Management, both at the University of Southern California. The list was composed of 70 academicians, 30 city planning officials, and 165 experts from the private sector in twenty states. I expected a return rate between 10 and 15 percent. The response rate was 22 percent. Sixty experts returned their questionnaires, and another eleven unanswered questionnaires came back due to unidentified addresses. (A full list of participants and the questionnaire appear in Appendixes A and B.)

Question 1 asked participants to rate their expertise in fields of urban design, urban economics, social impact of technology, and telecommunication technology. Question 2 measured household acceptance of several innovations ranging from telephones to fiber optic networks. Since most of the diffusion figures for the seven innovations (telephones, color television, VCRs, cable television, personal computer, mainframe terminals, fiber optic networks) are widely known from other research, these two questions are used to verify experts' knowledge for participation. I eliminated eight responses for inadequate proof of familiarity with the research area of investigation, and concluded with fifty-two responses for analysis see table 4.1). The respondents represent about 20 percent of their initial groups (fourteen academics, five public officials, and thirty-three business executives) from fifteen states.

I loaded the responses on a Lotus 1-2-3 spreadsheet file and ran a statistical analysis for the whole group and for each subgroup of academics, city officials, and private business in order to ground our analysis by magnifying any divergence or bias. The main analysis produced standard deviations, means, medians, minimum and maximum values, and frequency distributions.

The scope of change is the area under which change occurs. Because this area is determined by expertise and judgmental knowledge, there is no way to define the "best" judgment accurately. No one prediction is superior to any other. Therefore, the maximum and minimum values of variables have significance in determining the scope of future possibilities while the mean and standard deviation provide confidence in "the most possible" cases.

I divided the questionnaire into several sequential parts to investigate the propositions of chapter 3 about the telecity concept. The first part was directed to general knowledge about the diffusion of innovations and time allocation on a typical working day. This part, as described before, is designed to assist the verification of the participation of experts in the exercise. The second part asked direct questions about multilevel teleactivities: online economy, teleworking, and psychological neighborhood. Each

Table 4.1
The Characteristics of the Expert Group

Respondent Group	T	R	% T	% R
Academicians	67	14	20.90	26.92
Public Officials	28	5	17.86	9.62
Business Executives	159	33	20.75	63.46
Total	254	52	20.47	100.00

T = Total number of questionnaire sent
R = Number of successfully returned responses
% T = Percentage of responses to total number
% R = Percentage of subgroup to total number of responses

Total returned responses / questionnaire successfully received =
                          60/254 =   23.62 %

level included several questions to cover different aspects of the phenomena. The last part addressed location decisions, policy implications, and features of the general quality of life. The following is a summary of the results.

Most of the experts identified their field of expertise as communication technologies (1.5 on scale of 5), followed closely by social impact of technology (1.7), urban economics and location decisions (2.5), and finally physical planning (3.2). This composition of expertise prestructures the anticipated answers in the interpretation process.

Findings from table 4.2 highlight the rapid diffusion rate of several innovations in society through the year 2000. For example, expert consensus is that color television will reach 87 percent of households with only a 14 percent increase in ten years, while less developed technology such as fiber optics will be implemented at a faster pace of 400 percent in the same period (from 3.9 to 20 percent). Figure 4.1 illustrates that crucial innovations reflect a wide range of acceptance rates that affect the spread of teleactivities. Personal computers and two-way cable television are expected to reach 45 percent and 56 percent of the American households respectively by the year 2000.

Regular daily working hours will consistently decrease, while home-based work (such as teleworking) will steadily increase (from 1.3 to 2.6 hours). Table 4.3 shows that average daily commuting time will decrease significantly by the year 2000. This reduction indicates that remote communications are replacing the current physical movement in working activity, which is also confirmed in responses to questions 3, 5, and 11. Workers can tolerate longer commuting distance once they reduce the frequency of their journey to work. This result also explains that nonworking trips increase because extra leisure time is allocated to recreation, sports, and home entertainment.

Responses to the diffusion of teleactivities in the American households from 1990 to 2000 suggest that teleactivities are taking off, which necessitates careful consideration of their consequences on both households and city activities. These activities have a higher diffusion rate than first expected. Table 4.4, for instance, shows that American household engagement in tele-

Table 4.2
Diffusion of Selected Innovations

| Innovation | Year 1990 | | Year 1995 | | Year 2000 | | Rate |
	M	S.D.	M	S.D.	M	S.D.	1990-2000
Telephone devices	94.00	4.60	95.00	3.10	96.00	3.10	2.10%
Color Television	76.00	15.00	81.00	13.00	87.00	11.00	14.50
VCRs	50.00	13.00	59.00	13.00	68.00	14.00	36.00
Cable Television	40.00	12.00	48.00	11.00	56.00	14.00	40.00
Personal Computers	22.00	10.00	32.00	12.00	44.00	18.00	100.00
Terminals	7.00	6.30	11.00	8.50	18.00	13.00	86.00
Fiber Optics	3.80	4.20	10.00	8.90	20.00	16.00	526.00

Rate = rate of increase of these innovations from 1990 to 2000
M = Mean
S.D. = Standard Deviation

56

Figure 4.1
Mean Diffusion of Several New Information Innovations in the American Household, 1990-2000

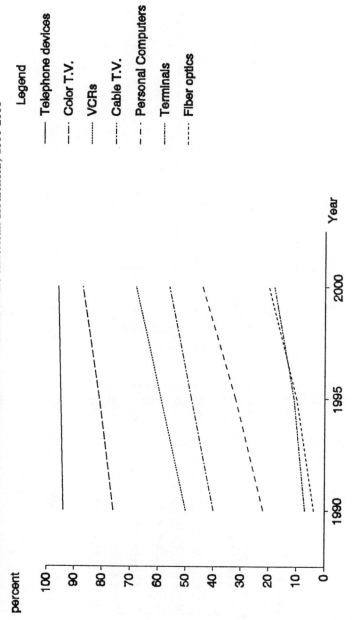

Table 4.3
Time Allocation for Managerial-Level Employees, 1990-2000

| Innovation | Year 1990 | | Year 1995 | | Year 2000 | | Rate |
	M	S.D.	M	S.D.	M	S.D.	1990-2000
Working Hours/Day	8.1	0.8	7.6	1	7	1.3	-14.00%
Home Based Work	1.3	0.5	2	0.9	2.5	1.2	48.00%
Entertainment	1.6	0.8	1.7	0.8	1.8	0.9	11.00%
Commuting	1.4	0.7	1.3	0.7	1.2	0.7	-14.00%
Social Relations	1.3	0.8	1.4	0.8	1.5	0.9	15.00%

Rate = rate of increase of these innovations from 1990 to 2000
M = Mean
S.D. = Standard Deviation

Table 4.4
Diffusion of Teleactivities in the American Household, 1990-2000

| TELEACTIVITY | Year 1990 | | | Year 1995 | | | Year 2000 | | | Rate |
	M	MD	S.D.	M	MD	S.D.	M	MD	S.D.	1990-2000
Online Economy	6.10	12.00	5.90	12.00	25.00	10.00	21.00	38.00	16.00	344%
Teleworking	6.20	7.60	3.50	11.00	13.00	5.90	19.00	23.00	10.00	307
Telebanking	8.60	15.00	7.90	18.00	25.00	12.00	28.00	38.00	18.00	325
ATMs	35.00	44.00	13.00	49.00	52.00	14.00	63.00	62.00	17.00	180

Rate = rate of adoption of selected teleactivities from 1990 to 2000
M   = Mean
MD   = Median
S.D. = Standard Deviation

59

activities can be expected to triple 1990 figures by 2000. ATMs will reach an average of 62 percent of common banking transactions (the highest score), while other conventionally transportation-based activities, such as teleworking, teleshopping, and telebanking, will involve 19 to 28 percent of American households. Figure 4.2 plots the mean rate of diffusion for some teleactivities: the online economy, teleworking, telebanking, and ATMs.

Although it is argued that the online economy is merely an electronic version of the catalogue department, it seems that neither this factor nor the expansion of the existing market are among the most significant features of online economy (table 4.5). The ability to reduce prices and the expansion of quality and variety of commodities offered to consumers indicate the benefits of the online economy (table 4.6). Diffusion of the online economy is heavily influenced by its costs: first, the running cost of monthly payments, followed by the initial costs of buying new information devices (table 4.7). It is important to note that activities included in a widespread online economy that require physical movement came first. Shopping, followed by banking, education, and entertainment are the most frequently used services (table 4.8). Thus, the online economy facilitates exchange of information and reduces transaction of commodities that require inconvenient or unnecessary trips.

The Delphi exercise emphasizes teleworking activity by addressing several questions. The results indicated a general consensus on increasing acceptance of teleworking in the American work force. While there will be an increase in nonworking trips, journey to work will decrease, which will have a positive impact on reducing congestion in central urban areas. Teleworking, the second layer of teleactivities, allows dispersion of residential areas, so that travel time and communication costs will have less influence on residence and business location decisions.

By the year 2000, on average 25 percent of the work force will be "frequent" teleworkers, those who engage one or more days per week in remote communication with their workplace by means of new information technologies. They will represent 42.4 percent of the total information-based activities workers. Table 4.9 indicates that the rate of increase of teleworkers in the ten-

Figure 4.2
Diffusion of Teleactivities in the American Household, 1990-2000

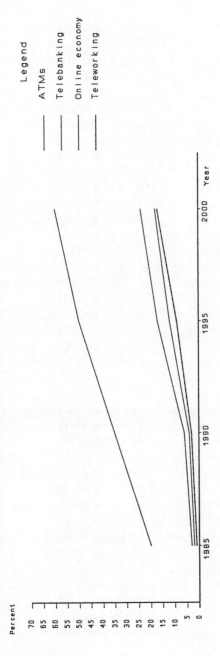

Table 4.5
The Impact of the Online Economy on Retail Business

Question # 6: How can the online economy influence the retail business ?
Least Important = 1
Very Important = 4

IMPACT	Total (52)		Acad (14)		P.O. (5)		B.E. (33)	
	M	S.D.	M	S.D.	M	S.D.	M	S.D.
Expand the Market	2.40	1.10	2.30	1.10	2.60	1.10	2.40	1.10
Replace Catalogue Department	2.40	1.00	2.30	1.00	2.40	1.00	2.40	1.10
Expand Geographical boundaries	2.80	1.00	2.80	1.00	2.80	1.10	2.80	1.00
Compete with Traditional Market	3.10	1.00	2.80	1.00	2.80	1.10	3.20	0.90

Total(52) = Total sample population (52)
Acad.(14) = Academic respondents (14)
P.O.(5)   = Public officials respondents (5)
B.E.(33)   = Business executives respondents (33)

M   = Mean
S.D. = Standard Deviation

62

Table 4.6
The Impact of the Online Economy on Consumers

Question # 7: Please indicate what the Online Economy offers to consumers
Least Important = 1
Very Important = 4

IMPACT	Total (52)		Acad. (14)		P.O. (5)		B.E. (33)	
	M	S.D.	M	S.D.	M	S.D.	M	S.D.
Reduce need for physical inspection	2.10	0.90	2.40	0.90	2.50	0.80	2.00	0.90
Expand quality & variety of commodities	3.00	0.80	2.90	0.80	3.60	0.40	3.00	0.80
Cheaper prices	3.00	1.10	2.10	1.10	3.20	0.90	3.30	0.90
No change	1.80	0.90	2.30	1.10	1.50	0.80	1.60	0.80

Total(52) = Total sample population (52)
Acad.(14) = Academic respondents (14)
P.O.(5)   = Public officials respondents (5)
B.E.(33)   = Business executives respondents (33)

M   = Mean
S.D. = Standard Deviation

63

Table 4.7
Diffusion of the Online Economy

Question # 8: To what extent does each of the following influence diffusion
of online economy (e.g. Dialog, CompuServe)?

Decrease = 1
Increase = 5

IMPACT	Total (52)		Acad. (14)		B.E. (33)	
	M	S.D.	M	S.D.	M	S.D.
Low Subscription fee	4.30	0.70	4.10	0.60	4.30	0.60
Number of services	3.90	0.80	4.20	0.70	3.80	0.80
Versatility of devices	4.00	0.90	4.30	0.70	3.90	0.90

Total(52) = Total sample population (52)
Acad.(14) = Academic respondents (14)
B.E.(33)   = Business executives respondents (33)

M   = Mean
S.D. = Standard Deviation

Table 4.8
Types of Teleactivities to Be Included in a Widespread Online Economy

Question # 9: Please check from the following list the candidate activity to be part of a wide spread online economy

Percent of the population indicating the use of these activities in an online economy

CANDIDATE ACTIVITY	% Total	% Acad.	% P.O.	% B.E.
Education	82	69	80	87
Entertainment	82	92	100	75
Business reports	92	100	80	90
News	74	76	80	71
Shopping	92	100	100	87
Communications	78	76	80	78

Total(52) = Total sample population (52)
Acad.(14) = Academic respondents (14)
P.O.(5)   = Public officials respondents (5)
B.E.(33)   = Business executives respondents (33)

Table 4.9
Composition of Information and Teleworkers

Question # 11: To your best estimate, what are the percentages in the following years of the labor force that will be engaged in information-based activities, and percentages of any sort of teleworkers.

Year	Type of Worker	Total (52)		Acad. (14)		P.O. (5)		B.E. (33)	
		M	S.D.	M	S.D.	M	S.D.	M	S.D.
1990	Information Workers	42.00	13.00	45.00	13.00	38.00	11.00	41.00	13.00
	Teleworker	11.00	9.20	9.30	8.60	15.00	10.00	11.00	9.00
	Ratio TW/IW	26.20%	–	20.70%	–	39.4	–	26.8	–
1995	Information Workers	50.00	13.00	52.00	11.00	46.00	14.00	50.00	13.00
	Teleworker	17.00	10.00	13.00	9.60	22.00	8.80	18.00	10.00
	Ratio TW/IW	34%	–	25%	–	47.80%	–	36%	–
2000	Information Workers	59.00	15.00	58.00	13.00	60.00	21.00	59.00	16.00
	Teleworker	25.00	14.00	21.00	15.00	29.00	4.40	26.00	14.00
	Ratio TW/IW	42.40%	–	36.20%	–	48.30%	–	44.10%	–

Increase in information workers (1990-2000)   = 140 %
Increase in Teleworkers (1990-2000)   = 227 %
Ratio of teleworkers as percentage of information workers = 162 %

Total(52) = Total sample population (52)
Acad. (14) = Academic respondents (14)
P.O. (5)   = Public officials respondents (5)
B.E. (33) = Business executives respondents (33)

M   = Mean
S.D. = Standard Deviation

year period (1990-2000) will be about 227 percent, higher than the rate of increase in information workers in the United States. I conclude that a larger proportion of information-based workers will be attracted to teleworking, and there will be a substantial increase in teleworkers. Journalists are the most likely, followed by scholars, professors, and professionals, to adopt teleworking (ranging from 95 to 84 percent frequency of responses) (table 4.10). Flexible working hours, the nature of the activity and product, and their high skills and educational background allow them to function under remote working conditions. The results are consistent with responses on questions 3, 5, and 15 (appendix B).

From table 4.11, large-scale companies will be able to absorb the initial expenses of implementing teleworking policy because of their ability to offer incentives. The large majority of the total responses (87 percent) indicates that these large-scale firms will be early adopters. Government agencies come in second place (53 percent of total responses), because teleworking will alleviate the demand for subsidies to support traditional transportation systems. But corporation headquarters and multinational companies still need centralized activities and communications in downtowns of large metropolitan areas, where small businesses, which demand face-to-face communications, have the lowest response rate of adopting a teleworking policy.

This analysis shows that the prospective use of new information technologies allows joint investment by public and private sectors in new types of information infrastructures that promote the intensive use of remote communication in data transmission (such as New York Teleport Project). Table 4.12 illustrates an increase of public spending on new information infrastructure and a tendency for savings in conventional transportation networks. Car ownership, on the other hand, will not be influenced by information technologies, since physical mobility between remote areas will still be a major component of transportation/communication linkages.

Social relations will be altered by new information technologies as this analysis emphasizes the impact of teleworking activity. One hundred percent of the responses indicate that teleworking attracts more part-time workers to the labor market while reducing total initial cost to organizations. But it is also important to stress that teleactivities will result in an emphasis on

Table 4.10
Occupations and Teleworking Adoption

Question # 10: From the following list, please check who are likely to adopt teleworking.

Percent of responses to qualify occupation to be engaged in teleworking

CANDIDATE OCCUPATION	% Total	% Acad.	% P.O.	% B.E.
Scholars	88	100	100	78
Professionals	88	100	80	84
Journalists	94	100	100	87
Administration	50	38	60	53
Executives	46	30	80	46

Total(52) = Total sample population (52)
Acad. (14) = Academic respondents (14)
P.O.(5)   = Public officials respondents (5)
B.E.(33)   = Business executives respondents (33)

Table 4.11
Teleworking and Business Organizations

Question # 13: Which of the following business organizations would most
likely to adopt incentives for teleworking?

Percent of responses to qualify business organizations to adopt
teleworking strategy

BUSINESS ORGANIZATION	% Total	% Acad.	% P.O.	% B.E.
Large-scale Company	89	100	100	83
Corporate Headquarters	38	30	40	41
Governmental Agencies	53	53	40	54
Small Business	36	38	20	38

Total(52)   = Total sample population (52)
Acad. (14) = Academic respondents (14)
P.O.(5)   = Public officials respondents (5)
B.E.(33)   = Business executives respondents (33)

Table 4.12
The Impact of New Information Technologies on Public Transportation Investment

Question # 12: Transportation projects of public sector, which intend
to reduce private inconvenience and costs, need increasing budgets
to meet demand for new and upgraded systems.
Please indicate which of the following statements you agree that
the use of information technologies allows:

Percent of responses agreeing to the statement

IMPACT	% Total	% Acad.	% P.O.	% B.E.
Reduction in conventional networks (freeways)	44	30	50	48
Increase in new infrastructure	53	70	25	51
Joint public and private investment (e.g., teleport)	79	90	50	79
Decrease in car ownership	23	40	25	17

Total(52) = Total sample population (52)
Acad. (14) = Academic respondents (14)
P.O.(5)   = Public officials respondents (5)
B.E.(33) = Business executives respondents (33)

family relations and home-centered activities, where leisure activities such as recreation and sports will also be enhanced (table 4.13).

Suburbanization, the expansion of metropolitan areas, is the most obvious impact of new information technologies on the urban pattern. Table 4.14 reveals that this prospect received 86 percent of the total responses. Decentralization, the distribution of economic activities and population, is the second impact on the urban pattern of new information technologies. Ruralization, the penetration of rural areas by city activities, has a moderate response rate of 58 percent. Finally, centralization (still an option for some activities such as corporation headquarters) enjoys the smallest impact of new information technologies on the urban pattern.

Several public policies are proposed in the questionnaire. Table 4.15 shows four public policy proposals for consideration to enhance the implementation of new information technologies. Standardization of communication and transmission technologies toward better connectivity and easier access enjoys almost a full consensus among the panelists with a mean of 9.3 out of 10. The application of different technologies makes communication more difficult and discourages adopting new technologies. For example, differing IBM and Apple operating systems for personal computers are still hurdles for many users to engage in office automation.

Deregulation of communication laws allowing expansion of broadcasting channels and other information services is the second most important policy with 7.4. Direct or indirect investing in public access to new information technology policy received a high grade of 7.3, emphasizing the importance of reaching those who benefit the least, given the wide diffusion of these services. The least important policy to be recommended is changing the current zoning policies toward mixed uses in residential areas. Although mixed activities will occur eventually, these activities are naturally integrated and generally quiet, clean working activities.

RESEARCH RESULTS

This Delphi exercise clarifies the complexity and future-oriented features of the impact of new information technologies on city

Table 4.13
The Impact of Teleworking on Social Relations

Question # 16: Do you agree that teleworking likely alters social relations in the following areas

Percent of responses agree on the statement

IMPACT	% Total	% Acad.	% P.O.	% B.E.
Increase family gathering at home	72	46	80	81
Enhance image of neighborhood	26	15	20	31
Introvert urban Areas	24	30	40	18
Increase leisure time	60	38	40	71
Active local centers	34	15	40	40
Reduce business costs	74	53	60	84
Employ more par-timers	100	100	100	100

Total(52) = Total sample population (52)
Acad.(14) = Academic respondents (14)
P.O.(5)   = Public officials respondents (5)
B.E.(33)   = Business executives respondents (33)

Table 4.14
The Impact of New Information Technologies on Urban Pattern

Question # 21: The impact of new information technologies may alter urban pattern toward (please check all applicable trends):

1) centralization (concentration of population and economic activities in few city centers).

2) decentralization (expansion of urban areas with distributed population).

3) ruralization (dispersion of economic activities to villages and small towns).

4) suburbanization (extension of emerging spotted residential areas in the outskirts of metropolitan cities).

Percent of responses agree on the statement

URBAN PATTERN	% Total	% Acad.	% P.O.	% B.E.
Centralization	36	41	33	32
decentralization	86	83	100	87
Ruralization	60	41	66	67
Suburbanization	91	100	100	83

Total(52) = Total sample population (52)
Acad. (14) = Academic respondents (14)
P.O.(5)   = Public officials respondents (5)
B.E.(33)   = Business executives respondents (33)

73

Table 4.15
New Information Technologies and Public Policy

Question # 23: Which of the following policies would you recommend
(with decandant order, very important=10) to exploit potentials
of new information technologies:

1) standardization of communication and transmission technologies for better
   connectivity and access.

2) deregulation of communication laws allowing wider expansion of
   broadcasting channels and other information services.

3) dezoning of the current limitations of land use policies toward mixed uses
   in residential areas.

4) investing, directly or indirectly, in providing public access to new
   information technologies.

PUBLIC POLICY	Total (52)		Acad. (14)		P.O. (5)		B.E. (33)	
	M	S.D.	M	S.D.	M	S.D.	M	S.D.
Standardization	9.3	1.5	9.1	1.2	10	0	9.2	1.7
Deregulation	7.3	2.2	6	2.5	4	1	7.9	1.8
Dezoning	4.5	2.6	5.4	2.7	4.3	2.4	4.2	2.5
Public access	7.3	2.4	8.4	2	8	0.8	6.8	2.6

Total(52) = Total sample population (52)
Acad. (14) = Academician respondents (14)
P.O.(5)   = Public officials respondents (5)
B.E.(33)   = Business executives respondents (33)

M   = Mean
S.D. = Standard Deviation

form. The variety of the experts' backgrounds and their scientific knowledge assured a diversity of responses that reflect the wide impact of the current social transformation. The Delphi exercise has achieved its objectives by demonstrating a tool that manages judgmental information to assess the impact of rapidly changing technology on a contextual problem—the city. The results validated several propositions. First, modern societies are experiencing changes in socioeconomic activities that depend on remote interaction (online economy and teleworking). Second, the exercise shows that these teleactivities are being adopted more rapidly in information societies such as the United States. Many firms, social institutions, and individuals are engaged in different types of information services, which requires adjustments to the new conditions in organizational structure, the control of information, and social behavior. Third, location decisions have been altered, and home-based activities will increase in the next twenty years. Fourth, the integration of these teleactivities in existing cities creates a situation of remote interconnectedness. The acceptance of teleactivities beyond critical mass by firms and public agencies is producing characteristics of the telecity. Fifth, decentralization of business and residential areas remains the major urban trend. Finally, appropriate public policies can encourage the rest of society to exploit potentials of new information technologies.

The validity of this research rests on five anchors: (1) the random selection of participants, (2) the large-scale recruitment plan from fifteen states, (3) representation of a wide array of expertise, (4) the high rate of return of the questionnaire, and (5) the high unanimity among the main group as well as the three subgroups in the main propositions of the research. Their deviations occur on issues related directly to their individual expertise, so that the likelihood of arriving at the same result as any other group of expertise is high. Moreover, the evaluation of the exercise is founded not only on explanation of empirical results but essentially on an understanding of the research propositions, reflecting a shift from reliance on empirical data to the essential logical connections.

This exercise achieved its main objective in confirming the high diffusion rate of teleactivities in the present information society and potential future trends.

The next chapter examines the impact of the emerging telecity on the main theories of urban form. The sequel should produce a conceptual model about the telecity.

NOTES

1. Although forecasts are part and parcel of policymaking and the requirement to prepare them is written into laws and government regulations, little attention has been given in the field of planning to advance the use of appropriate techniques.

2. We have to bear in mind that all forecasting is normative. It is neither value-free nor assumption-free. Forecasts rely on values, perception of the future, and visions of experts and analysts.

3. Some writers have described planning as a process involving the preparation of a set of decisions that can be adapted to the environment in a way that is consistent with prevalent goals and values (Ingelstam 1977, 127-145).

4. Policymaking is fundamentally a future-oriented action. Planning intends to influence future events and change the perceived problems of the present. Future studies can support decision making by supplying information relevance in a long-range perspective.

5. For elaborate discussion about inquiry systems, see Churchman (1971).

5

Telecity:
A Theoretical Analysis

The previous chapters argued that our societies are facing a fundamental transformation process caused by new information technologies. New activities characterized by remote interactivity have emerged. These teleactivities enjoy an increasing rate of adoption and have direct impact on the quality of urban life as the telecity concept is emerging.

In this chapter the impact of new information technologies on social transformation—therefore on city form and structure—is examined through the analysis of three perspectives about city form: the physicalist, the urban economist, the sociologist.[1]

The physicalist perspective tends to minimize the significance of social relations, and concentrate on the physical elements of the city. Urban elements such as schools, hospitals, and public spaces shape urban life. The main conviction of the physicalist claims that human beings are strongly affected by the physical features of their environment. It is the process of manifesting social structures into symbolic expressions.

The economist perspective perceives the city as a practical machine. It emphasizes efficiency, the close support of activities, good access, and easy repair or remodeling. Activities are located according to their relative cost of reaching labor, materials, markets, and services (Wingo 1961; Alonso 1964; Muth 1969).

Competition for space within the city results in high land rents near the center, where communication costs are low and access high, and low rents near the edge of the settlement. The arrangement of land uses, rents, and therefore land values explains the concentration of businesses and professional activities in the center of the urban area, the central business district (CBD), leaving the periphery to residential uses.

The third perspective is concerned with the social meaning of the city, referring to spatial structure as a reflection of the society's dominant culture. To understand the city, analysis of the basic components of the society (including its institutions and population) is necessary. Even for some scholars, such as Wiener and McLuhan, society can be understood only through the study of messages and communications facilities.

These perspectives do not share the same stage of theoretical development. For instance, the economist's perspective started in the 1820s. The physicalist perspective is also well developed, originating from Ebenezer Howard's concept of the Garden City in the 1890s, to the City Beautiful Movement, to Kevin Lynch and modern theorists of urban design. The social meaning perspective is the least developed because of its recent involvement in urban studies. The first two perspectives will be presented in their "conventional wisdom" context, and the third through the study of three major theorists: Castells (1983a, 1983b), Rogers (1983), Meyrowitz (1985), and Rapaport (1984).

The following section will explain these perspectives and suggest the most likely changes in their assumptions and the emergence of new propositions. After that, this chapter will conclude by establishing a theoretical framework to construct a conceptual model for the telecity.

THE PHYSICALIST PERSPECTIVE: THE IMAGE OF THE CITY

Designers and physical planners view the city through its materialistic time–space relationships within social symbolism. City form is the result of various configurations of these relationships expressed in everyday city life. Lynch (1960), who established the conceptual basis for the study of urban design, identified the five basic components of physical form. The visual analysis of a place is expressed in terms of paths, edges, nodes, districts, and landmarks.

Paths accommodate mode and sense of movement. While moving through them, people observe the city (street patterns and transportation networks). Along them, other physical elements are arranged and related to interactions and social behavior. Urban patterns, generally referred to as paths, consist of the network of habitual or potential lines of movement through the urban complex, and as such, are the most potent means of achieving an ordered whole.

Nodes are strategic foci that are typically junctions of paths or places for important activity. Because directional decisions must be made at a junction, people pay greater attention to such places and perceive nearby elements with more clarity than normal. Nodes are most important in metropolitan regions in arranging the entire region perceptually into a static hierarchy in which every part focuses on minor nodes. Districts, edges, and landmarks characterize the image, but they play the least role in arranging the image of the city as a whole.

Elements of city form overlap and penetrate one another. None exists in isolation, but always in relation to its surroundings. These physical elements compose a "language" to understand and manipulate the urban environment. To be considered a visual element, an object should exhibit a sense of oneness, structured with other elements, and have meaning to the city inhabitants. The perceived elements and their various structures construct the cognitive schema that identifies the city. City form is reflected in our minds as mental maps. Nearly every sense is in operation, and the image is the composite of them all (Lynch 1960, 2).[2] Most often, our perception of the city is partial, fragmented, and mixed with other concerns. As the product of both immediate sensation and the memory of past experience, this image is used to interpret information and guide action. A legible city would be one whose elements are easily identified and easily grouped into an overall pattern (Lynch 1960). The image of the city is the collective overlapped images of individuals.

Since the image of the city is a temporal creation, the change of perception occurs with any new state, mood, or type of activity practiced by the city's inhabitants. Speed of action and purpose of movement may alter the observer's perception in gathering urban elements to create a modified image of the environment. A vivid example is the invention of cars. When the automobile was marketed, the image of our cities was completely transformed in two ways: (1) perception was altered by the change in the speed of movement in new and larger areas, and (2) wider street patterns and expensive transportation networks replaced narrow, winding paths suitable for pedestrians.[3]

The Image: A Nodal Structure

Basic physical elements such as paths, edges, nodes, districts, and landmarks will not change with new information technologies. Their physical impacts are limited to adding some details to buildings (satellite dish receivers). The real impact of new information technologies is their ability to improve accessibility through the same transportation, provide more spaces for business activities, expand city limits, and relocate business to allow mixed uses. The multiplication of these impacts influences the creation of the collective image of the city.

New information technologies that permit dispersion of residential areas and workplaces in such a large interdependent region allow images to merge with our experience. Change in perception of the physical environment is the result of changes in interaction with city function. The relation beween activity and its spatial location is weakened. The perception is constructed by the virtual network of habitual connectedness among various points only in time of interaction. The sequence of events is based not on their relative closeness, but rather on their functional integration.

Nodes become the most important element in the image of the telecity. The image will depend mainly on the experience of its population through places of interaction rather than through movements in city paths. Nodes become the main components in structuring the image on places of action. The image will be related to the perceived image of location according to the customized observer. To enhance the visual image of the city, it is crucial to concentrate activities in nodes and public spaces. Environmental interpretation is dominated by the perception of virtual location of teleactivities.

As the conceptual anchor points in telecities, a series of nodes can form a related structure. The essence of such elements is in their distinct, unforgettable "place," with intensity of use strengthening its identity. A whole pattern will be sensed and developed by sequential experiences. This pattern creates a sense of interconnectedness at any level of interaction and in any direction. A sense of place is not locational, but rather virtual in everybody's mental map, which entertains a flexible interaction and an adaptable schema to changes in perception. In short, the image of the telecity does not depend on physical path patterns or hierarchical nodes, but rather on versatile nodal structures in analogy to neurological nodes in the brain. If some are blocked, an alternate exists.

THE URBAN ECONOMISTS' PERSPECTIVE: CENTER OF ACTIVITY

The analysis of the city as the center of activity has a long history that has produced the most coherent body of social theory to date (Thünen 1966; Christaller 1966; Lösch 1954). Cities are patterns of activity in space that facilitate the production, distribution, and consumption of goods. The primary idea is that space imposes an additional production cost—time and resources—on movement through it.[4] Thus, economic activities are arranged for the most efficient outcome depending on transportation and communication relationships.[5]

Cities represent the spatial concentration of people and, consequently, economic activity (Richardson 1978). Business, the core of these activities, is usually located in the most accessible areas of the city CBD. Around these centers, cities are shaped to form the city structure.[6] Since most citizens commute from homes to work occupying street patterns, transportation is costly and time consuming (Lynch 1984).

Different distances from the CBD reflect a wide variation in production activities due to affordability of accessible land. The price of land changes with distance whereas the price of other inputs remains stable. Consequently, the more accessible the land, the higher is the rent. Thus, the lower rent areas are left to residential uses (Wingo 1961; Alonso 1964; Meier 1962; Muth 1969). Accordingly, the individual must allocate a portion of his location budget to trade off between transportation/communication costs and rent.[7] This analysis also explains the variation in building types over the metropolitan area, with highrise office buildings near the center, while low-density single-family houses are on the periphery. This efficient distribution contributes to city form and its skyline.

Urban economists have often neglected the role of technology in shaping social settings. Since Johann Von Thünen, they have assumed linear movement of residents and goods, scarcity of urban land, and the dominance of political power over means of production in a capitalist market (Lake 1983).

Virtual Networks: A Nonhierarchical Structure

New information technologies alter conditions of accessibility of information and goods, and, thus, flexibility of location decisions. New telecommunication networks create an interactive electronic system to connect nodes of various activities. "Electronic highways" stand as the main infrastructure, which spatially rearranges both industrial locations and business offices. New information technologies create potential to manage, reorganize, and control dispersed tasks and link processes of production, distribution, and management. This change implies (1) relaxation of the home–work relationship; (2) dispersion of manufacturing processes; (3) reduction of face-to-face communication in selected occupations; and (4) a decreasing number of journeys to work with the opportunity to relieve congestion. Telecommunication channels and various levels of teleactivities allow the transmission of information to remote areas, offering greater flexibility in the location of economic activity. On the other hand, these technologies allow both the centralization of decision making and interconnection of dispersed individuals despite their physical separation. The communication–transportation trade-off is becoming feasible.

New information technologies do not substitute linear movements in the city; they only shift locational relationships to nonlinear networks. While they do not displace existing infrastructure, they suggest a declining burden of public and private expenditure to maintain and operate the existing networks. They influence choices of locations among a complex of socioeconomic factors. Improving accessibility to markets has changed the structure of land use and allowed mixed and multiple uses.

In the information society everyday activities will tend to concentrate in residential areas. Public spaces accommodate these activities in a decentralized structure and play host to teleworking remote centers and public access to teleactivities. These spaces construct a skeleton for the expansion of the urban fabric and further diffuse economic activities to remote areas. The mix of work and leisure time in residential areas of the information society creates integration among services, entertainment, and recreation. The creation of decentralized local centers suggests a nonhierarchical structure.

Hierarchical centers assume "lower" and "higher" functions distributed in the city ranging from local centers to regional shopping centers. Each level of service has different functions that coincide and serve a specific geographical domain. Higher centers accommodate higher service levels covering several lower-level services. City inhabitants refer to each level according to their need to acquire levels of services. But teleactivities reverse this process by the flexibility of moving from one level to another instantly. The accessibility of different service levels from homes or local centers creates a new order independent of instance or assigned service area where they continuously overlap. The local center, which may have a general catchment range, creates an appropriate neighborhood environment for social interaction among part-time workers, teleworkers, and the handicapped. Family surveillance, security, and neighborhood safety will be assured by a strong concentration of activities.

THE SOCIAL MEANING PERSPECTIVE: INTERPRETATION

In this perspective, "city" implies an emphasis on the practices and ideas that arise from collective and individual experiences that constitute urban life and form. Urban form is not only an expression of society but also, according to Castells (1983), a fundamental material dimension of society; thus, to consider it independently of social relationships is to separate nature from culture.

This perspective is the most recent approach to the study of urban form and structure. It is not yet a conventional wisdom. Several theories have been developed that offer an interpretive format for the effects of new technology. The first is drawn from the tradition of historical materialism based on the struggle for social meaning among conflicting interests. The second relies on communications studies emphasizing situational behavior, the diffusion of innovation. The third is from the school of cultural geography.

Social Meaning: A Political Struggle

Castells' (1983a, 1983b) central thesis identifies the basic tendencies of the historical struggle over the definition of urban meaning. The city is a social product resulting from conflicting interests and values, and the particular spatio-temporal forms they take are among the most vivid structures conditioning human action (Giddens 1981). Social processes relate economic factors and technological progress, which play a major role in establishing the meaning of urban space, to appropriate spatio-temporal forms and social organizations to their environment. Social processes are relentlessly challenged by the production of new values and the emergence of new social interests.

Since this theory views the city as a long-term historical sequence, it admits the presence of many overlapping and contradictory features, which are either relics of the present or early manifestations of the future (Lynch 1984, 341). City form is the residue and the sign of conflict. Thus, cities are historical products, not only in their materiality but in their cultural meaning. Urban meaning is not mental representation of a spatial form; it is the assignment of structural tasks to this form in accordance with the conflicting social dynamics of history.

Castells argues that under the current conditions the meaning of places in people's consciousness tends to disappear. The spatial project of the new dominant class tends to disconnect people and spatial form, and therefore, people's lives and urban meaning. Each city derives its actual social meaning from its location in the hierarchy of networks whose control will be in the hands of technocrats. Social meaning dissolves in each place and from the people of each place. The new resource of power relies on the control of the entire network of information in which activities are dissolved into flows of information. The new attempted urban meaning is the spatial and cultural separation of people from their product and from their history. However, this emerging spatial form is always challenged by alternative urban meaning projected by the rest of the society, particularly labor.

Urban Experience: A Delocalization Process

New technologies induce the delocalization of private life as they do for work-oriented organizations. Homes become disassociated, but in the meantime connected with neighborhoods and cities. Homes no longer need to be lonely, isolated places. The residential landscape becomes decentralized and individualized while, at the same time, information systems strengthen the importance of few places, where the location of many activities cannot be transformed into flows (Castells 1985).

In the telecity, spatial singularity and urban centrality become even more important for high-level managerial functions, thus concentrating on specialized education institutions, recreation areas, specific production centers, and special face-to-face delivery activities (from hospitals to boutiques). Telecity centers become the matrix for nesting the most important activities of the psychological neighborhood.

In this view, the main spatial impact of the new technology is the transformation of spatial places into flows and channels, which amounts to the delocalization of production and consumption. The social collective meaning is dissolved in the geographical landscape with its perception and interpretation facing conflicting forces: the majority of individuals who struggle to construct their cognitive maps against those who control information. It is an old scheme with new players—information versus capital of the industrial analysis.

The impact of teleactivities and the emergence of the telecity magnify the interpretation process of urban meaning. Two modes of social meaning are always in progress: the social meaning of conflicting interests, and the social meaning of a continuing value system in the reproduction of urban meaning.

Communication: Sense of Place

Meyrowitz (1985) developed communication theory that addresses the role of new communication technologies on the physical aspect of society. His theory is based on Goffman's (1959) and McLuhan's (1964) concepts of social behavior. He argues that human behavior is socially determined by the situation confined by both place and time of interaction. People adhere to a complex matrix of conventional behavior and maintain their performance in each ongoing situation without undermining different behavior in other social situations. When communication and travel were synonymous, distinguishing between situational behavior patterns was simple.

A place defines a distinct situation because its boundaries limit our perception and interaction. We behave differently depending on the social situation. Moving from classroom to movie theater, for example, allows for orderly transitions from situation to situation and from one behavior pattern to another.

Telecommunications: New Sense, Behavior, Activities

Meyrowitz (1985) argues that there is a change in the "sense of place." The evolution of media and new information technologies has decreased the significance between physical place and social "place." The logic of situational behavior has changed with the human senses and their technological extensions in new patterns of information flow, leading to two changes: (1) changes in social position and physical location, which allow the dissociation of social situations from their confinement; and (2) changes in perception, by extending the senses, and changes in the "sensory balance" of people, which alter their behavior patterns and perception.

The theory of diffusion of innovations (Rogers 1983) augments the argument of change in social behavior. Diffusion of new information technologies results in a selective contact change in which society's exposure to innovation is spontaneous or incidental. Those receiving information are left to choose, interpret, adopt, or reject the new idea. Their adoption and interpretation of innovations alter behavior, leading to changes in activities. Further diffusion of these ideas to other members of society through communications creates processes by which alteration can occur in the structure and function of an entire social system. Therefore, changing ideas can become quickly reflected in social activities.

New information systems change both perception and social activities. Perception is the way in which external stimuli are subjectively interpreted or experienced by an individual according to background, experience, and behavior (Rogers and Burdge 1972). Perception of a visual form depends on the social meaning the observer associates with the object, which can also be altered according to his interactive link to a "seamless" web of nonlocational places. Change is the social meaning associated with places (home, theater, classroom) as spheres of physical situations overlap. New information technologies remove the physical barriers impertinent to social information.

New information technologies accelerate the adoption of new innovations, the interpretation of their uses and meaning, and the communication processes to other adopters. By influencing individual preference and social behavior, these processes alter social activities—those held in public spaces become less important, as people prefer the convenience of home and less interaction with the city's physical environment. For example, VCRs increasingly usurp the importance of cinema, theaters, and concerts, as such entertainment activities can now be enjoyed with family or friends in the privacy of home.

The emergence of new social activities is a natural response to changing societal relations. The increase of leisure time and interactive communication in society promise to generate new leisure-time activities, travel, and tourism, which might involve small groups but will certainly affect function and use of space. Changes in social activities forces changes in the city form, the physical

setting for these activities. A place for integrated social interactions, local centers offer a suitable environment for people to
adapt to such changes.

The City: Cultural Context

In contrast to the physicalist approach, Amos Rapoport's
(1969, 1984) conception of city form is that the relationship
between culture and different urban orders is manifested in the
landscape, for the worldview shapes the urban scene. Culture is a
set of values and beliefs from which we develop characteristic
ways of viewing the world. Urban morphology can only be interpreted sensibly in its cultural context. By contrast, conventional
reliance on the market as an allocation mechanism or transportation technologies as determinants to explain form, a view held by
urban economists, appears misleading.

Cities are physical artifacts, experienced through their inhabitants' senses while moving sequentially through their spaces.
Cities as particular forms of organization can be understood by
four variables in experiential order: space, time, meaning, and
communication. Environmental order, in this sense, goes beyond
the order expressed in the built form.

Telecity: Superimposed Orders

In Rapoport's view (1984), meaning in modern cities is pluralistic, deriving from different cultures, and thus less lexical and
more idiosyncratic than the traditional situations. In modern
metropolitan areas with massive populations and intensive social
interaction, redundancy and more explicit cues contribute in
articulating urban form to diverse groups with varied and
mutually incomprehensible codes. Consistent use of certain sets of
cues is essential to communicate through social space. This
redundancy factor is often achieved by "superimposing" new kinds
of systems over the spatial order. Distinct, explicit, and complex
information systems and their meaning are systematically added
to spatial, locational, and other systems, so that the urban

environment is an expression of (and modular of) activity systems in a cognitive schema. City form is a signifying system with symbolic meaning that is absorbed by city dwellers and visitors, who then act upon these meanings. Dramatic changes in city morphology and social patterning generate new sets of meanings, so that the city has a role in the genesis of culture and is not a mere product of culture.

The explanation of the four city forms of space, time, meaning, and communication is best tailored to the new conditions of the telecity model. The nonlocation of several services with instantaneous connectivity alters the location relationships of places as well as changes the pluralistic meaning. Communication among these information-active places (nodes) creates a higher order of interconnection to link experience and mobility in a cognitive schema. Based on distributed nodes, a cognitive schema strengthens social meaning in the basic information order. The process of interpreting activity locations of overlain meanings and linkages creates a superimposed structure of virtual communication networks. Designation of activities to virtual location and their disassociation with specific spaces constitute a landscape of many "shadows" of the place.

The three theories of social meaning concur that meaning is an interpretation process that conceives social reality whether it is conflictual, situational, or contextual. The image (locational and superimposed) is a fundamental part of human consciousness permitting purposeful mobility by relating the self to the environment. While the image is valuable in this immediate sense, it can also serve as a general frame of reference within which the individual can act, or to which he can attach his knowledge.

Conceptual Model of the Telecity

Three perspectives have been examined to illustrate the impact of new information technologies and the emergence of teleactivities on city form and structure. Each perspective produced unique concepts to explain the current changes. Since each acts in a separate domain of knowledge, the outcomes supplement each other by indicating changes to be expected in the physical image of the city, location decisions, and interpretation of city life.

First, the image of the city will shift in the sense that many activities in diverse places act as if they are located in proximity. Telecity, as such, is "superimposed" over the physical city (or cities)—it is hard to perceive activities in their spatial structure from within the city.

Telecity centers are symbolic points around which a loosely patterned countryside is organized. They become the focus of regional identity where intensified natural features strengthen that symbolism. These centers of stimulus and decision are continuously active. Probably, most of them are outgrowths of earlier central places.

Second, the pedestrian city boasts an intimate mixture of land uses, identified as "functional integration." Any block, or single building, was likely to house people as well as provide manufacturing, selling, or storage space. Improved urban transportation produced "natural segregation," allowing workers to live away from their workplace. The journey to work was lengthened from meters to kilometers, but the time spent in travel remained nearly constant for most passengers (Pederson 1980). The integration of functions may recur if work, housing, and services mix in the same place, an illegal situation in most present-day cities, since it violates zoning ordinances based on the "natural segregation" of incompatible activities.

Third, city life is, in large part, a life lived through symbols. Possessions—both the hardware of city elements and the software of information, knowledge, beliefs, and ideas—become precious in exact ratio to their expressiveness, their capacity to define the relationship of the self to the city (Raban 1974). The need to display cognitive locations of activity is a stable reflection of self in loose activities and identities.

As the city has become more complex and faceless, its inhabitants depend more and more on explicit information to interpret and explain activities and their locations. As cities decentralize and grow, individuals will never experience more than a part of the city, so two possibilities arise: either individuals nest in their neighborhoods and localities where they have stronger image and control of their boundaries, or superimposed images will support and strongly tie city components and activities, simply enough, to the customized individual.

Thus, in each of the three perspectives, space has a central position due to the advancement of information technologies. First, it becomes the focus of the visual image of the city in which observers perceive the built environment in nodal hierarchical patterns built around spaces. Second, it becomes the place for concentrated activities and services in delocalized, multinodal structures, nesting mixed uses, information services, new places of production, and teleworking centers in which leisure and work are mingled. Third, it serves as a social gathering place where diffusion of innovations and an exchange of ideas, behavior, and culture are accommodated. The versatile role and associated functions of spaces make them essential to identify levels of distributed structures. It becomes more difficult to identify the real location unless multilevel structures are apparent with high rates of redundancy.

NOTES

1. Since the beginning of systematic study of society, social scientists have been interested in the quest for social change. However, they have studied social transformation processes without much notice of the spatial configuration of that change.

2. Image is based on knowledge of the environment. Messages about this environment consist of information, which are structured experience which endows them with meaning to produce changes in the image (Boulding 1969). The environment, then, is a language of communication, with a syntactic and semantic structure.

3. For a complete account of changes in city patterns, see Morris (1972). Use of the gridiron system is not exclusive for the post-automobile city. Greek and Roman cities were dominated by the "mesh" of paths.

4. Christaller's (1966) central place theory and that of Lösch (1954) claimed that services are distributed according to hierarchical and spatial pattern. Earlier, Thünen (1966) provided the land rent model, in which land rent differentials over space are explained solely by access to consumers, or in other words, transport cost savings.

5. These theories are static, although restorative changes occur after every shift in resources or when obstacles to free market play are imposed or removed.

6. Some types of arrangement are central, linear, polycentric, multi-centric, or spread city.

7. The same hypothesis of distance to CBD and intensity of use at close-in location which reflects rents of lands is the basis for several models. Alonso (1964) developed the seminal model of location, which states that iso-profit function showing how a firm's willingness to pay for urban site varies with distance from the CBD in order to guarantee the same level of profit anywhere in the city. The trade-off model of residential location indicates that households trade off accessibility for space in making their residential site choices. Muth's model (1969) shows that a negative exponential pattern of gross population densities in relation to distance from CBD is a close approximation to actual patterns of population distribution and, therefore, locations for their services.

6

Telecity Form and Structure: Review and Conclusion

The development of a structure of centers containing major spaces for activities is the basis for elaborating on the telecity concept, which has been derived from the previous three perspectives. Telecity centers are modules for the new city structures. They are the arrangement by multiple levels to articulate space in a large and complex environment. Yet, they impose an extra burden of organization on the observer, especially if there is little relation among these levels. Telecity centers' dependence on virtual networks, which connect the superimposed structure to the city inhabitants, and the interpretive process of teleactivities location require a high degree of redundancy in common elements to link different levels of structures cognitively.

A distribution of these structures can be abstracted as an arrangement of focal points (or nodes) with a special character. The pattern can be seen as a network, with a form in itself, a degree of connectedness, a scale, and a degree of specialization. This multinodal nonhierarchical pattern accommodates multipurpose or highly specialized activities, and accordingly, information flows peak at these points or broadly disperse. When describing flows and flow facilities, a network description is clearly appropriate and applies to other kinds of linkages: social, economic, or even visual (Lynch 1984, 357). Along with focal organization, network description is one of the prime ways in which people tend to organize their images of the city.

City life is structured both spatially and temporally (Berger and Luckmann 1967, 26). Spatial structure is manifested in locational relationships of activities in the physical dimensions of the city. The temporal structure, as an intrinsic property of consciousness, is far more important. Every individual is conscious of the inner flow of time; even location is related to the sequence of events along his movement. Time is the fourth dimension in a flow of city elements and location of activities that create the perception of the city (Lynch 1960). Superimposed structures of the telecity form a temporal structure. It depends only on the asynchronous interactive communication of activities with little link to their location. It is possible to differentiate between different levels of this temporal structure, as it is intersubjectively available. Therefore, the telecity is manifested as structure on a spatial frame, which is quite peripheral to our perception and to several individualized temporally superimposed structures.

Structures of the telecity are not hierarchically ordered in subordinated systems. Instead, they are interrelated and interpretively distinct on different levels of social interaction. While they do overlap, each structure is composed of interrelated elements.

The *basic structure* consists of the telecity center, which becomes the core of the neighborhood in which its activities are centered. It encompasses most of the integrated functions of the city while providing intensive, highly specialized information systems to its citizens. Its electronic mall includes huge commercial, retail, and service data bases accommodated in virtual networks. The application of these technologies alleviates some inherited problems by decreasing work trips and mixing residential and business uses. Improved education, social services, and citizen interaction will require more decentralized centers featuring live and recorded audiovisual aids and information terminals for public education.

Specialization in the functions of decentralized centers becomes less important since it is inconsistent with the capabilities or characteristics of the new information systems, which have relaxed locational constraints. However, this concept does not preclude the importance of creating an identity for each telecity center derived from its environment and citizen feedback.

The telecity center concept differs from the satellite center concept in that it fragments organizations instead of relocating them. A firm would rent office space in distributed telecity centers scattered throughout the residential landscape and allow each employee to work at the center nearest to his or her home. Thus, a unit of a few employees would probably be working in different centers. And since the concept depends on employee location rather than workplace, it certainly requires an extensive telecommunication network. If this concept works, depending on innovative organization and information systems, it will have the tremendous advantage of allowing people to live where they choose and work where telecenters exist (Harkness in Golany 1976). The ultimate solution, of course, is working totally out of the home. Teleworking offers a further step to scatter these nodes into every house.

The *topological structure* is composed of three levels of innovation—at homes, electronic kiosks, and telecity centers, which are organized to meet the diverse needs of telecity citizens for easy and convenient accessibility. First, *homes*, the nest for the information revolution, are where many electronic devices (cable television, personal computer, telephone, VCR, etc.) are integrated into an interactive center to perform various flexible functions—from home security and energy control to a global reach, while for the telecity, the diffusion of home integrated system digital network (ISDN) units is the basis for city development. Second, *electronic kiosks*, similar to public phones, are the intermediate transition innovation to accommodate the fluctuation and flexible usage of information services and are distributed in the city fabric. These kiosks include the ATMs, videotext, computer terminals, and communication channels in a simple usable machine. Third, *telecity centers* contain similar interactive ISDN units for the public use. These communication hubs also include higher specialized and sophisticated equipment for particular and customized uses—teleconferencing, electronic mail facility, tele-education centers, and local bulletin boards.

The *technology structure* identifies three levels of technological innovation in the telecity centers, where (1) *infrastructure* innovations include receivers and antennas, transmitters, coaxial cable and fiber optics networks, television stations, mainframe computers, and control units; (2) *communication channels* innovations include all media, telephone cable lines, and personal computers for two-way interactive networks; and (3) *information services* consist of the applications of software and programs to conduct new facilities for information exchange, which are housed in videotext, teletext, and electronic mall data base. Terminals for the interactive access to these systems are located in telecity centers, kiosks, and homes.

The *information services structure* is composed of location- and non-location-specific services. Location-specific services are related to identified features of the site (geographical, historical) and add special sense and function to the center. For example, an onshore "marine telecenter" might contain marine recreation facilities and aquarium knowledge functions. Location-specific services represent a higher level of services to meet specific demands on the national or world scale and become the network source to connect and transmit its specific function via information systems. The multinodal structure of location-specific services in telecity centers creates very sophisticated networks, and travel to the telecity's location is necessary only for education and interaction.

The non-location-specific services are those activities located in every telecity center. (1) General decentralized services establish the social welfare facilities, such as education institutions, health centers, social facilities, and the local teleworking center. They are physical components of the telecity center and are linked by transportation networks. (2) The virtual network of information service provides the surrounding residences with electronic places for teleactivities such as teletext and videotext terminals for convenient public demonstration.

The *spatial hierarchical structure* involves overlays of *locational structure*, where the hierarchical relationship is the basic physical network. The observer perceives the city not according to distance factor but the relative location between these centers. Since many activities should have a physical access, transportation networks create a multinodal physical structure for private and public transportation. The *superimposed structure* of communication technologies connects each citizen interactively with services in the convenience of his home, office, or telecity center. The individual will have a superimposed perception of the relationship of these services regardless of their actual locations. The integration of these perceptions to a level of structural relation will enrich a vivid image of the telecity. Superimposed structures will customize many places (or functions) to individual needs. Its flexibilty and connectivity are crucial to the functions of every center and enhance the image of the telecity.

The *site planning structure* mandates that the telecenters should be designed as human environments with close social relations among their users. Inner, semi, and open spaces require a human scale to accommodate these interactions: huge front spaces and high confinement violate the relaxed sensation of proportions suitable to the scale of the activity. The functions of telecity centers will, accordingly, depend on the quality of design and specific location characteristics to attract more participants to create livable places.

TELECITY CENTERS AND HUMAN INTERACTIONS

One advantage of the telecity center is its customized services and firms, which can adjust to individual need by applying different configurations of information technologies. It offers the motivated individual easy access, low-cost, intensive, highly configured information systems to connect to other individuals in interactive networks. The range of services includes interaction among individuals for social purposes and connecting organizational business to international firms. The process of information exchange allows people who share interests to fulfill their talents and, at the same time, creates a suitable dynamic atmosphere for innovation. The possibility of choosing residence location regardless of workplace location strengthens individuality by providing every individual with an international reach for information, knowledge, and innovation. Telecity centers function as windows on the globe.

On the other hand, high-tech industries and business firms that can benefit from new possibilities of separating their production phases can relocate in telecity centers according to each firm's business strategy. They can isolate administration work for low-wage, part-time employees at home and so reach a wider labor market with specialized qualifications.

Citizen Participation in the Telecity

Improved communication between citizens and political institutions is the basic attribute of public participation in political decision-making processes. Emerging new information technologies make possible a rich information context, keeping the politically interested citizen abreast of the changing political scene at federal, state, and local levels. He can access information about a topic, a policy, or a national issue. He may be able to interconnect on a local or national scale, debating with other interested individuals to clarify the issues. Citizenship under such circumstances becomes a more active, aggressive process. Interactive communications can endow citizens and their political institutions with knowledge, expertise, and insight (informative function) (Fathy et al. 1986).

On the other hand, new information technologies alter the technological rigidities and lag in the political institutions, which limit where and how often citizens can vote. Voting could take place electronically from home terminals or from public terminals in distributed telecity centers. This electronic process will open opportunities for more direct democracy. Qualified voters could access by means of "smart cards" or passwords, which could be matched to voter registration lists and verified. In the "voting booth" (home terminals or the public electronic access), the voter would have access to various levels of information that would help him reach more knowledgeable decisions.

Thus, the interactive capabilities of the new information technologies would allow citizens to inquire and receive advice about government. Public hearings could take place at the computer virtual network, and formal notice could be taken of each citizen's participation. At the same time, government officials could elicit information from the citizenry as a constitutive panel.

Thus, new information technologies offer opportunities to endow that critical element of political structures—the citizen's vote—with a vastly enriched information environment. Furthermore, these technologies free the relationship from historical time–place constraints, transforming participation from a casually informed political act to continuous interaction between citizens and their political institutions. And highly developed two-way communication service is an essential prerequisite for new forms of direct democracy to emerge.

Having followed the logic of elaborating on structures of the telecity, and having anticipated some potentials of new information technologies on the quality of the telecity nodes, the study arrives at its conclusion of the main proposition.

TELECITY: RETROSPECT AND PROSPECT

This study has provided an approach to investigate the current social transformation processes and their impact on city form and structure. New information technologies have played a dialectical role in the development of current events. First, they assist in the generation, processing, management, and control of information, which is increasingly strategic in socioeconomic activities. Modern society depends on information-based activities as the major economic sector in both gross national product and labor force. Second, they further diffuse information to larger populations who engage in interactive communications for their work, services, and facilities.

The intertwining relationships in the shift of economic activity and the use of interactive communication have foreshadowed changes in urban life:

1. Relaxation of constraints of location decision provides increased flexibility in the location of both economic activities and residence. Reduced congestion and average daily commuting distance as well as an increase in nonworking trips are anticipated as a result of teleworking. Other telecommuting activities, such as telebanking and teleshopping, are following the same rate of acceptance.

2. Land values have become less dependent on distance to CBDs, and geographical and local characteristics are more important in determining real estate value. Teleactivities have relaxed transaction costs of information, reducing the competition among economic activities for valued locations in the city and extending the labor market to more part-time workers, women, and handicapped from both local and remote areas.

3. "Back-office operations" of large corporations in remote

neighborhoods may be spatially dispersed and functionally related to the main office without losing efficiency. The diversion of interdependent economic activities of production, marketing, management, and distribution processes to remote locations allows scale economies without urban concentration.

4. The revitalization of neighborhoods and local centers involves the natural integration of work and leisure at homes; the nonwork trips to daily shopping for food and recreation and the increase of part-timers return the focus of local centers to neighborhood residences. The distributed remote teleworking centers in neighborhoods further enhance the use and image of urban spaces. People will gather more often for face-to-face communication involving leisure, recreation, sports, and performing tele-activities such as telebanking from public access.

5. Regarding the cosmopolitan characteristics in the hypertemporal spatial landscape to reach-out work, services, and information, individuals extend their senses to access news, media, entertainment, and information about a variety of interests. They are part of the global economic, social, and political interdependence among regions and countries. The new international division of labor is one example of the new international relations.

6. A more active political participation by the citizenry has emerged within each level of the democratic processes.

Subsequently, city form and structure have undergone changes in (1) the image of the city to a nodal structure of concentrated local activities, (2) the spatial arrangement of economic activities and residential areas, and (3) individual interpretation of city activities. A superimposed image is created in every individual, which manifests his interactive engagement of teleactivities generating multilayer nonlocational cognitive maps.

The telecity concept is a product of the information society. Since Western societies are becoming more dependent on information-based activities, and these activities can take advantage of the qualities of new information technologies for their development, the emergence of teleactivities fosters the transformation process. Society's exposure to new information technologies will generate several integrated levels of teleactivities. A telecity emerges when a critical mass of society is engaged in remote services, facilities, and work in everyday life. New technology liberates traditional spatial-temporal constraints, increasing the potential of current technological change. Thus, cities can choose from any number of strategies to alleviate inherited problems and match the transformation processes with innovative solutions.

The telecity concept produces a multinodal, nonhierarchical structure to accommodate teleworkers engaged in teleactivities, and provide information services to both its inhabitants and other customers. Linear physical movement within the city's transportation system has been complemented by superimposed multi-dimensional mobility on virtual networks.

The centrifugal force of decentralization clusters location-specific activities for local spaces in a large geographical area. Local space plays an important role in the life of future cities. As technology makes telecenters more attractive and city transportation networks less onerous, private cars become more desirable and low density living areas more available.

This study has shown that one of the fundamental dimensions of technology is its interpretive quality. New information technologies reveal the ability of society to "see" through the type of technology in use. Technology is socially determined, and the use of new information technologies differs in each social context. For instance, computers liberate not only our actions, but the way we think and process those actions. In every society there are changes that can be moderated by new forms of technology; the more interpretive its dimension appears, the greater the changes in behavior and values. New social behavior patterns and new social institutions are created that later become commonplace experience. Realization of new liberties and creation of new social institutions mean social change. This conclusion suggests why technological transfer, particularly to Third World countries, is so difficult.

To arrive at such conclusions, this study had to pass through several stages of specifying the relationship between technology and society and its impact on the form and organization of the city. The first stage established the concept of technology and its historical role in the evolution of industrial society. The second stage provided a general map of socioeconomic activities of production and consumption in an information society. The integration of production sectors and diffusion of new information technologies generate such teleactivities as online economy and teleworking. The aggregation of these activities on a city scale produces the telecity, where social interactions, services, and work depend on interactive, individualized, and asynchronous technologies.

The third stage developed a technique to validate the previous propositions by using a version of the Delphi method. This exercise provided a consensual statement of the opinions of multi-disciplinary experts and applied these changes to the future. The fourth stage explained critical changes in city form through three perspectives: those held by physicalists, urban economists, and scholars of social meaning. It proposed a theoretical model of a multinodal nonhierarchical structure designed to accommodate most of the current changes in city form. Finally, it projected overlaid, distributed structures.

The study reveals the value of using futures research methodologies in planning. The use of a novel Delphi version made it possible to validate propositions about the impact of teleactivities on social life and to project these consequences into the future within a wide range of expectations. The use of this nonpositivistic, unorthodox method is appropriate to analyze planning research questions within a rapidly changing environment, with hard-to-obtain data, and with a multidisciplinary approach.

The study and its analyses have paved the way for several policy implications. New information technologies will have greater social effects, especially when accompanied and supported by the public policies essential to match social changes with social institutions. Four public policies have been discussed in the Delphi exercise, all of which demonstrate the critical role of new information technologies. Further investigation of these public policies is essential to assure their appropriateness. The four policies are: (1) standardization of communication and transmission technologies toward better connectivity and easier access; (2) deregulation of communication laws allowing wider expansion of broadcasting channels and other information services; (3) investing, directly or indirectly, in public access to new information technologies policy, especially the least bene-fited members of society with respect to wide diffusion of these services. The public sector holds a vital stake in assuring that individuals and firms within a city have access to advanced infor-

mation technologies; however, unlike other urban infrastructures, the private sector has been the primary instrument for
the construction of telecommunications infrastructure in large
American cities; and (4) the least important policy recommended
in the Delphi exercise is changing the current zoning policies
toward mixed uses in residential areas. Although mixed activities
will occur eventually, these activities are naturally integrated and
generally quiet and clean working activities.

New information technologies require other research efforts to
collaborate with this study. The study of new technology is still in
its infancy, much like transportation planning in the mid-1950s.
Case studies of specific cities and further investigation of public
policies and implementation strategies are needed most. New information technologies are not only ignored in the design of new
communities, they are largely neglected in the study of old ones.
Telecommunications should be included in designing for the
future.

The challenge is to determine under what conditions the centralization or decentralization processes would occur, the types of
cities likely to benefit or be damaged by the deployment of
advanced information technologies, and public policy alternatives for cities seeking to harness these technologies to achieve
progress. Nevertheless, the impact of new information technologies on urban form will depend on the extent to which people will
need to visit city centers for work or services, and how well the
centers can compete with teleactivities and the more peripheral
collections of shops, services, or employment. The patterns of settlement are determined by other factors that direct people to
employ new information technologies according to the city structure and their way of life.

Appendix A:
List of Panelists

Robert Annunziata, President, Teleport Communications, Inc., New York

Gary Arlen, Arlen Communications, Inc., Bethesda, Maryland

Gene Bell, Director, Pacific Bell, San Ramon, California

Carrie Bennett, Senior Project Manager, Transamerica Information Services, Los Angeles, California

August H. Blegen, Association of Data Communication Users, Bloomington, Minnesota

Daniel Brenner, Communication Law Program Director, University of California–Los Angeles, California

Virgil J. Carden, Director Plant Communications, Dow Jones & Company, Inc., Princeton, New Jersey

Thomas V. Chema, Chair, Public Utilities Commission of Ohio, Columbus, Ohio

Ken Coleman, Deloitte Haskins & Sells, Los Angeles, California

Theodore S. Connelly, Communications Institute, San Francisco, California

David P. Cook, ComQuest Company, Cincinnati, Ohio

Martin Cooper, Chairman, Cellular Business Systems, Park Ridge, Illinois

Robert Crawford, Vice President, Biola University, La Mirada, California

Karen R. Davidson, Chair, Business and Social Science Division, University of Redlands, Redlands, California

Burnie Dunlap, Vice President, Communique Telecommunications, Inc., Ontario, California

John Edwards, Los Angeles County, Los Angeles, California

T. E. Farmer, Vice President, Rockwell International Telecommunication, Dallas, Texas

Marshall M. Feldman, Cleveland State University, Cleveland, Ohio

Michael Ford, Director, British Telecom International, Inc., New York

Michael Freedman, Telecommunication Supervisor, Quotron Systems, Inc., Los Angeles, California

Amy Glasmeier, University of Texas at Austin, Austin, Texas

Britton Harris, Professor Emeritus, University of Pennsylvania, Philadelphia, Pennsylvania

Frank Hotchkiss, Senior Vice President, Southern California Association of Governments, Los Angeles, California

Robert Jacobson, Principal Consultant, Assembly Committee on Utilities and Commerce, Sacramento, California

Cherie S. Lewis, University of California–Los Angeles, Santa Monica, California

Will Lorey, Director of Management Development, Northern Telecom, Richardson, Texas

Lee McKnight, Program on Communication Policy, MIT, Cambridge, Massachusetts

Lawrence A. McLernon, President and CEO, LCI Communication, Inc., Worthington, Ohio

Edward Malecki, Associate Professor of Geography, University of Florida, Gainesville, Florida

Donald A. Marchand, Dean, School of Information Studies, Syracuse University, Syracuse, New York

Gary Martin, Market Research and Analysis Manager, General Telephone Company of California, Los Angeles, California

Robert L. Mathews, District Manager, Bell Communications Research, Piscataway, New Jersey

Robert H. Meixner, Arthur Andersen & Co., Chicago, Illinois

Susan Mersereau, Manager of Telecommunications, Weyerhaeuser Company, Tacoma, Washington

Douglas J. Mitchell, Consultel, Wayland, Massachusetts

Mitchell L. Moss, New York University, New York

Vincent P. Murone, President, Communique Telecommunication, Inc., Ontario, California

Jack Nilles, University of Southern California, Los Angeles, California

Kevin C. O'Brien, Division Manager, Bell Communication Research, Red Bank, New Jersey

Michael O'Neal, Director, Northern Telecom Inc., Nashville, Tennessee

Edward A. Otting, Director of Information Systems Operations, Eli Lilly & Co., Indianapolis, Indiana

Alan Pearce, President, Information Age Economics, Bethesda, Maryland

Paul Polishuk, Information Gatekeepers, Inc. Boston, Massachusetts

James Rothenberger, Senior Manager, Carter Hawley Hale, Anaheim, California

Edwin A. Schreiner, Corporate Director, Strategic Marketing/Planning, White Plains, New York

Al Sharif, District Manager, AT&T, Los Angeles, California

Howard Shaw, Shaw Communications Consultants, Miami, Florida

Barbara S. Shields, District Manager, AT&T Communications, Los Angeles, California

Donald Siebert, Siebert Telecommunication Consulting, Inc., Overland Park, Kansas

Christopher H. Sterling, George Washington University, Washington, D.C.

Arlo Woolery, Executive Director, Lincoln Institute of Land Policy, Cambridge, Massachusetts

Peyton Wynns, Chief of Industry Analysis Division, FCC, Washington, D.C.

Appendix B:
The Delphi Exercise

THE QUESTIONNAIRE

STATISTICAL ANALYSIS

5-res-11-23-87

RESEARCH DESIGN

THE IMPACT OF NEW INFORMATION TECHNOLOGY ON CITY FORM

This research aims at a dynamic design process of the form and structure of the city in the future under the impact of new information technology. This exercise attempts to exploit expectations for 10-20 year time horizon under the rapidly changing technology in the United States using the Delphi technique

The Delphi Exercise is a sensitive method to anticipate potentials of what the city of the future would look like within the complex societal impact of technology. This research investigates the spatial arrangement of activities and their structural patterns. The judgmental data generated from expert opinions will be systematically analyzed to judge the research propositions about potentials and direction of the current technological impact.

A list of 300 panelists is selected from scholars, private business experts, and city planners to cover a wide array of expertise familiar with both fields of new technologies and urban setting.

Because of the multidisciplinary nature of this research, this questionnaire may not exactly match your experience. **Please answer those questions you feel comfortable with.**

The Questionnaire

----

1. From your wide interests and experience, please indicate all areas of expertise starting

   by the closest to your field of specialization = (1):

a) Physical planning/urban design   ( )

b) location decision making/transportation   ( )

c) social impact of technology/ communications   ( )

d) telecommunication technology   ( )

e) others: ----------------------------   ( )

2. To the best of your knowledge, what is the percentage of diffusion of the following

   innovations in American households by the following years:

innovation	% of HH by	1990	1995	2000
a) telephone devices		------	------	------
b) color TV		------	------	------
c) VCRs		------	------	------
d) cable TV		------	------	------
e) personal computers		------	------	------
f) terminals to mainframes		------	------	------
g) fiber optic networks		------	------	------

3. To the best of your knowledge, how will time be allocated in an typical middle class

professional working day to each of the following activities:

	1990	hr.	1995	hr.	2000	hr.
a) regular working hours	—		—		—	
b) home-based work	—		—		—	
c) recreation and sports	—		—		—	
d) home entertainment	—		—		—	
e) shopping	—		—		—	
f) commuting	—		—		—	
g) social relations	—		—		—	

4. If houses accommodate more economic and socioeconomic activities,

how can you anticipate the change to each of the following:

	1990	1995	2000
a) reduce housing space per person			
b) more mix activities in living spaces			
c) decrease work space per person at work			
d) increase recreation and open spaces			

5. What is the anticipated percentage of American households that are engaged

in the following activities :

% of HH by	1990	1995	2000
a) online economy	-------	-------	------
b) teleworking	-------	-------	------

c) remote social communication	-------	-------	------
d) teleconferencing	-------	-------	------
e) telebanking	-------	-------	------
f) ATMs	-------	-------	------

6. How can online economy influence the retail business? Please scale the following in

   (least important = 1; very important = 4):

a) create new lines and expand the existing market ( )

b) replace catalogue departments ( )

c) expand the geographical boundaries of small business ( )

d) compete with conventional retailbusiness ( )

e) increasing threats for less overhead and inventory expenses ( )

7. Please indicate what the online economy offers to consumers

   (least important = 1; very important =4)

a) reduce the need for physical inspection of some goods where superior

information about goods could be obtained ( )

b) expand the reach for quality and variety of commodities ( )

c) cheaper prices (due to decrease in inventory, low rent, and overhead costs) ( )

d) no significant change because shopping is basically an entertaining activity ( )

8. To what extend does each of the following influence the diffusion of online economy (e.g., Dialog, CompuServe):

	decrease			increase	
a) low subscription fee	1	2	3	4	5
b) large number of services in	1	2	3	4	5
single channel					

c)versatility of devices for other   1 2 3 4 5

   activities (telephone network,

   TV broadcasting, Cable TV, and PC)

9. Please check which of the following services can be compiled

   to a widespread online economy

a) education (general education, open university,..)   ---

b) entertainment (reading materials, games,...)   ---

c) business reports (financial reports, banking ..)   ---

d) news (local,international, weather,..)   ---

e) shopping   ---

f) communication (electronic mail, subject clubs,..)   ---

g) others: _____   ---

10. From the following list, check all who are likely to adopt teleworking

a) scholars and professors   ( )

b) professional   ( )

c) journalists and writers   ( )

d) administration and clerical workers   ( )

e) executives and high managerial level   ( )

f) others : _____   ( )

11. To your best estimate, what is the percentage of the labor force who will engaged in information-based activities, and percentage of any sort of teleworking in the following years:

	information workers	teleworkers
a) 1990	%	%
b) 1995	%	%
c) 2000	%	%

12. Transportation projects of the public sector to reduce private inconvenience and costs still need budgets for the increasing demand for new and upgrading the current systems. Please indicate with which of the following statements you agree. The use of new information technologies allows:

a) reduced public investment in conventional networks   ----

b) increased public spending on new infrastructure   ----

c) shift toward joint public and private investment

   in new information technologies (such as teleports)   ----

d) decreased car ownership   ----

13. Which of the following organizations would most likely adopt incentives for teleworking:

a) large-scale companies   ( )

b) corporation headquarters   ( )

c) governmental agencies   ( )

d) small business (1 - 500 employees)   ( )

14. Teleworking, as an example of telecommuting activities, has strong impacts on:

	week	strong
a) less dependence of residence on work location	1 2 3 4 5	
b) allow mixed uses of residence and work	1 2 3 4 5	
c) dispersion of services to remote areas	1 2 3 4 5	
d) increased role of local centers	1 2 3 4 5	

15. How do you assess teleworking impact on city transportation system?

	1990	1995	2000
a) decrease congestion	__%	__%	__%
b) decrease trip generation	__%	__%	__%
c) decrease concentration of business activities in CBD	__%	__%	__%
d) increase commuting distance between home and work unit	__%	__%	__%

16. Do you agree that teleworking is likely to alter social relations in the following areas:

a) increase family relations and home centered activities	( )
b) enhance neighborhood unity and image	( )
c) isolate urban areas toward introvert activities	( )
d) increase leisure and relaxation time	( )
e) create social and recreational activities around local centers	( )
f) reduce total initial costs for organizations (saves in working space, site cost, parking areas,...)	( )
g) bring more part time workers to the labor market	( )

17. To the best of your knowledge, what is the percentage of typical employees today who favor teleworking strategy

a) preserve the current working conditions   %

  (reject teleworking)

b) split working hours   %

c) full-time telecommuting   %

18. From your investigation, what is the average distance from home among

    the following members of your social group:

                                miles

a) work colleagues' residences

b) family friends

c) relatives (in the same town)

d) work place

19. What is the percentage of out-of-town frequent communication

    for the following activities

	1990	1995	2000
a) services	--%	--%	--%
b) work- related	--%	--%	--%
c) friends	--%	--%	--%
d) family members	--%	--%	--%

20. According to spatial variation of level of services, please show where

the following activities are likely to be nested in the year 2000:

                                          LSS   NLSS   TCC   SC   CBD

a) primary school

b) retail stores

c) work space

d) corporation headquarters

e) remote teleworking center

f) online economy main computer

g) online economy public access

h) entertainment

     LSS: Location-Specific Services;

     NLSS: Non-Location Specific Services;

     TCC: Telecity Centers;

     SC: Small Cities;

     CBD: Central Business District of large cities

21. The impact of new information technologies may alter the urban pattern toward

(please check all applicable):

a) **centralization** (concentration of population and activities in few city centers)   ( )

b) **decentralization** (expansion of urban areas with distributed population)   ( )

c) **ruralization** (dispersion of economic activities to villages and small towns)   ( )

d) **suburbanization** (extension of the current trend in industrial societies of

emerging spotted residential areas in the outskirts of metropolitan cities)   ( )

22. Can you define any geographical area that could be considered now an example of

"telecity" (where remote services, facilities, work, and social relation dominate city life):

_____

if not when -----------

23.Which of the following policies would you recommend (with a descendant order,

very important = 10) to exploit potentials of new information technologies:

a) **standardization** of communication and transmission technologies

   to better connectivity and access   ( )

b) **deregulation** of communication laws allowing wider expansion

   of broadcasting channels and other information services.   ( )

c) **dezoning** of the current limitation of land use policies toward

   mix uses in residential areas   ( )

d) **investing,** directly or indirectly, in providing public access

   to new information technologies   ( )

24. Please write any comment that is not covered in your answers:

Abbreviations

TOT = Total Population of the exercise (52 panelist)

A   = Academicians (14 panelists)

P   = Public officials (5 panelists)

B   = Business Executives (33 panelists)

Stan = Standard deviation

Max   = Maximum value

Min   = Minimum value

Med   = Median

AVG   = Average value (Mean)

SUM   = Toatal value of the column

% R   = Percentage of responses to the column

Q #   = Question number (refer to the questionnaire)

Table A.1
Panelist Expertise Composition (Question 1)

Total Population (52)

Q # 1	A	B	C	D	E
Stan	1.40	1.00	0.70	0.80	1.10
Max	5.00	4.00	3.00	4.00	5.00
Min	1.00	1.00	1.00	1.00	0.00
Med	3.00	2.50	2.00	2.50	2.50
AVG	3.20	2.40	1.70	1.70	1.70
SUM	58.00	52.00	74.00	26.00	26.00

Academicians (14)

	A	B	C	D	E
Stan	1.30	1.20	0.80	0.60	1.40
Max	5.00	4.00	3.00	4.00	5.00
Min	1.00	1.00	1.00	2.00	1.00
AVG	3.50	2.10	1.80	2.50	1.80
SUM	25.00	17.00	20.00	23.00	11.00

Public Officials (5)

	A	B	C	D	E
Stan	1.60	0.40	0.90	1.20	0.00
Max	5.00	3.00	3.00	4.00	1.00
Min	1.00	2.00	1.00	1.00	1.00
AVG	2.20	2.20	1.80	2.60	1.00
SUM	9.00	11.00	9.00	8.00	2.00

Business Executives (33)

	A	B	C	D	E
Stan	1.10	0.80	0.60	0.30	0.90
Max	5.00	4.00	3.00	2.00	3.00
Min	1.00	1.00	1.00	1.00	1.00
AVG	3.40	3.00	1.70	1.10	1.80
SUM	24.00	24.00	45.00	38.00	13.00

Table A.2
Diffusion of Several New Information Technologies in American Households (Question 2)

Total Population (52)

YEAR	a			b			c			d			e			f			g		
	90	95	20	90	95	20	90	95	20	90	95	20	90	95	20	90	95	20	90	95	20
Stan	4.6	3.2	3.1	16	13	11	14	14	14	13	12	15	11	13	18	6.4	8.6	13	4.3	8.9	17
Max	100	100	100	96	97	100	80	85	95	61	70	80	50	70	90	25	35	50	20	40	80
Min	80	85	85	40	45	50	15	20	30	10	20	25	5	7	10	1	1	1	0	0	1
Med	90	93	93	68	71	75	48	53	63	36	45	53	28	39	50	13	18	26	10	20	41
AVG	94	96	97	76	82	87	50	59	68	40	49	56	23	33	44	7	12	19	3.8	10	20

Academicians (14)

	a			b			c			d			e			f			g		
	90	95	20	90	95	20	90	95	20	90	95	20	90	95	20	90	95	20	90	95	20
Stan	2.4	2.1	1.7	16	14	13	13	13	12	8.2	9.5	11	10	12	18	5.3	6.9	8.1	5.7	14	25
Max	99	100	100	95	97	98	70	80	90	55	65	80	50	60	75	20	22	25	20	40	80
Min	90	93	95	40	45	50	20	30	45	30	35	37	10	15	18	1	1	1	0	1	1
AVG	95	97	98	79	83	88	50	60	67	43	52	58	24	35	45	5.3	8	12	4.5	12	21

Public Officials (5)

	a			b			c			d			e			f			g		
	90	95	20	90	95	20	90	95	20	90	95	20	90	95	20	90	95	20	90	95	20
Stan	1.3	2.6	5.1	14	10	8.2	10	11	13	4	8	17	7.1	7.7	16	5.8	6.9	8.2	0	0	0
Max	95	96	97	96	97	98	60	65	80	50	60	80	35	40	70	15	30	50	20	20	40
Min	92	90	85	65	70	75	30	35	40	40	40	30	15	20	25	1	2	3	20	20	40
AVG	94	95	94	84	88	91	45	56	63	42	49	54	25	35	48	7	15	21	20	20	40

Business Executives (33)

	a			b			c			d			e			f			g		
	90	95	20	90	95	20	90	95	20	90	95	20	90	95	20	90	95	20	90	95	20
Stan	5.4	3.5	3	16	13	10	16	15	15	15	13	16	11	14	19	6.7	8.3	13	3.5	6.1	12
Max	100	100	100	95	97	100	80	85	95	61	70	80	50	70	90	25	35	50	15	30	60
Min	80	85	88	40	45	50	15	20	30	10	20	25	5	7	10	1	2	2	0	0	1
AVG	94	96	97	74	80	86	51	60	69	39	48	55	21	31	43	7.7	13	21	3.4	9.2	19

122

Table A.3
Time Allocation (Question 3)

Total Population (52)

YEAR	a			b			c			d			e			f			g		
	90	95	20	90	95	20	90	95	20	90	95	20	90	95	20	90	95	20	90	95	20
Stan	0.9	1.1	1.3	0.6	1	1.3	0.8	0.9	1.2	0.8	0.8	0.9	0.4	0.4	0.4	0.7	0.7	0.7	0.9	0.9	0.9
Max	10	10	10	3	5	6	5	6	8	4	4	4.5	2	2	2	5	5	5	4	4	4
Min	6	5	4	0	0.5	0.5	0.3	0.5	0.5	0.5	0.5	0.5	0	0.1	0.1	0.5	0.5	0.5	0.2	0.2	0.2
Med	8	7.5	7	1.5	2.8	3.3	2.7	3.3	4.3	2.3	2.3	2.5	1	1.1	1.1	2.8	2.8	2.8	2.1	2.1	2.1
AVG	8.1	7.6	7.1	1.4	2.1	2.6	1.2	1.3	1.5	1.7	1.81	1.8	0.7	0.8	0.8	1.4	1.3	1.3	1.4	1.4	1.5

Acadimics (14)

	a			b			c			d			e			f			g		
	90	95	20	90	95	20	90	95	20	90	95	20	90	95	20	90	95	20	90	95	20
Stan	0.9	0.9	1.3	0.5	0.8	1.4	0.5	0.5	0.6	0.8	0.8	0.8	0.4	0.4	0.4	1.1	1.1	1.1	1	1	1
Max	10	9	9	2	3	5	2	2	2	3	3	3	1	2	2	5	5	5	3	3.5	3.8
Min	7	6	5	1	1	1	1	0.5	0.5	1	0.5	0.5	0.3	0.3	0.3	0.5	0.5	0.5	0.2	0.2	0.2
AVG	8.4	8	7.6	1.4	2	2.7	1.2	1.2	1.4	1.9	2	2.1	0.7	0.8	0.8	1.6	1.5	1.5	1.6	1.5	1.5

Public Officials (5)

	a			b			c			d			e			f			g		
	90	95	20	90	95	20	90	95	20	90	95	20	90	95	20	90	95	20	90	95	20
Stan	0.9	1.4	1.9	0	0.5	0.5	0.3	0.1	0.5	0.5	0.5	0.5	0.4	0.4	0.4	0.4	0.4	0.5	0	0.3	0.4
Max	9	9	9	2	2	2	1	1	2	2	2	2	1	1	1	1	2	2	1.5	1.5	1.8
Min	7	6	5	1	1	1	0.8	0.3	1	1	1	1	0.3	0.5	0.3	1	1	1	1	1	1
AVG	7.7	7	6.3	1	1.7	1.7	0.8	0.9	1.3	1.5	1.5	1.5	0.7	0.8	0.8	1.5	1.5	1.3	1	1.3	1.4

Business Executives (33)

	a			b			c			d			e			f			g		
	90	95	20	90	95	20	90	95	20	90	95	20	90	95	20	90	95	20	90	95	20
Stan	0.8	1.1	1.2	1	1	1.2	1	1.1	1.5	0.8	0.8	0.9	0.4	0.4	0.4	0.5	0.5	0.5	0.8	0.8	0.9
Max	10	10	10	3	5	6	5	6	8	4	4	4.5	2	2	2	2	2	2	4	4	4
Min	6	5	4	0	0.5	0.5	0.5	0.5	0.5	0.5	0.5	0.5	0	0.1	0.1	0.5	0.5	0.5	0.5	0.5	0.5
AVG	8.1	7.6	6.9	1.4	2.1	2.6	1.2	1.4	1.6	1.7	1.7	1.7	0.7	0.8	0.8	1.2	1.2	1.2	1.4	1.4	1.5

Table A.4
Diffusion of Teleactivities in American Households (Question 4)

Total Population (52)

YEAR	a 90	a 95	a 20	b 90	b 95	b 20	c 90	c 95	c 20	d 90	d 95	d 20
Stan	1.69	1.68	1.71	0.92	0.79	0.8	1.49	1.48	1.47	1.62	1.47	1.49
Max	5	5	5	5	5	5	5	5	5	5	5	5
Min	1	1	1	2	2	2	1	1	1	1	1	1
Med	3	3	3	3.5	3.5	3.5	3	3	3	3	3	3
AVG	3.44	3.59	3.65	4.55	4.65	4.68	3.69	4	4.05	3.78	4.06	4.11

Academicians (14)

	a 90	a 95	a 20	b 90	b 95	b 20	c 90	c 95	c 20	d 90	d 95	d 20
Stan	0.5	0.5	0.5	1	0.83	0.83	0.82	0.5	0.5	1.89	1.41	1.41
Max	2	2	2	5	5	5	5	5	5	5	5	5
Min	1	1	1	3	3	3	3	4	4	1	2	2
AVG	1.5	1.5	1.5	4	4.25	4.25	4	4.5	4.5	3.67	4	4

Public Officials (5)

	a 90	a 95	a 20	b 90	b 95	b 20	c 90	c 95	c 20	d 90	d 95	d 20
Stan	1.73	1.96	1.73	0	0	0	2	1.73	1.96	0	0	0
Max	5	5	5	5	5	5	5	5	5	5	5	5
Min	1	1	1	5	5	5	1	1	1	5	5	5
AVG	2	2.6	2	5	5	5	3	2	2.6	5	5	5

Business Executives (33)

	a 90	a 95	a 20	b 90	b 95	b 20	c 90	c 95	c 20	d 90	d 95	d 20
Stan	0.92	0.81	0.77	0.99	0.85	0.9	1.29	0.96	0.8	1.61	1.6	1.64
Max	5	5	5	5	5	5	5	5	5	5	5	5
Min	3	3	3	2	2	2	2	3	3	1	1	1
AVG	4.4	4.5	4.64	4.55	4.67	4.7	3.89	4.5	4.6	3.36	3.73	3.82

Table A.5
The Impact of Online Economy (Qeustions 6-8)

Total Population (52)

	On Retail Business				Consumers advantage				Diffusion		
Question	Q # 6				Q # 7				Q # 8		
	a	b	c	d	a	b	c	d	a	b	c
Stan	1.153	1.077	1.084	1.013	0.97	0.818	1.13	0.994	0.761	0.832	0.925
Max	4	4	4	4	4	4	4	4	5	5	5
Min	1	1	1	1	1	1	1	1	2	1	1
Med	2.5	2.5	2.5	2.5	2.5	2.5	2.5	2.5	3.5	3	3
AVG	2.46	2.4	2.84	3.12	2.196	3.065	3	1.814	4.306	3.959	4.041

Academicians (14)

	Q # 6				Q # 7				Q # 8		
Stan	1.146	1.146	1.099	1.099	0.929	0.828	1.167	1.106	0.662	0.799	0.722
Max	4	4	4	4	4	4	4	4	5	5	5
Min	1	1	1	1	1	1	1	1	3	2	3
AVG	2.385	2.385	2.846	2.846	2.462	2.923	2.154	2.333	4.154	4.231	4.308

Public Officials (5)

	Q # 6				Q # 7				Q # 8		
Stan	1.02	1.02	1.166	1.166	0.866	0.49	0.98	0.866			
Max	4	4	4	4	3	4	4	3			
Min	1	1	1	1	1	3	2	1			
AVG	2.6	2.4	2.8	2.8	2.5	3.6	3.2	1.5			

Business Executives (33)

	Q # 6				Q # 7				Q # 8		
Stan	1.172	1.057	1.064	0.909	0.964	0.823	0.92	0.867	0.698	0.82	0.962
Max	4	4	4	4	4	4	4	4	5	5	5
Min	1	1	1	1	1	1	1	1	2	1	1
AVG	2.469	2.406	2.844	3.281	2.034	3.036	3.345	1.63	4.355	3.806	3.903

Table A.6
The Impact of Teleworking (Questions 9-10, 12-13)

	Activities included in Online Economy Service	Early Adoptors of Teleworking	Advantages of Info. Tech.	Organization Acceptance

Total Population (52)

Q # 9

Q. #	a	b	c	d	e	f	g
Freq.	41	41	46	37	46	39	2
% R.	82	82	92	74	92	78	4

Q # 10

	a	b	c	d	e	f
Freq.	44	44	47	25	23	3
% R.	88	88	94	50	46	6

Q #12

	a	b	c	d
Freq.	19	23	34	10
% R.	44	53	79	23

Q # 13

	a	b	c	d
Freq.	44	19	26	18
% R.	90	39	53	37

Academicians (14)

Q # 9

	a	b	c	d	e	f	g
Freq.	9	12	13	10	13	10	0
% R.	69	92	100	77	100	77	0

Q # 10

	a	b	c	d	e	f
Freq.	14	13	14	5	4	0
% R.	100	100	100	38	31	0

Q #12

	a	b	c	d
Freq.	3	7	9	4
% R.	30	70	90	40

Q # 13

	a	b	c	d
Freq.	13	4	7	5
% R.	100	31	54	38

Public Officials (5)

Q # 9

	a	b	c	d	e	f	g
Freq.	4	5	4	4	5	4	0
% R.	80	100	80	80	100	80	0

Q # 10

	a	b	c	d	e	f
Freq.	5	4	5	3	4	0
% R.	100	80	100	60	80	0

Q #12

	a	b	c	d
Freq.	2	1	2	1
% R.	50	25	50	25

Q # 13

	a	b	c	d
Freq.	5	2	2	1
% R.	100	40	40	20

Business Executives (33)

Q # 9

	a	b	c	d	e	f	g
Freq.	28	24	29	23	28	25	2
% R.	88	75	91	72	88	78	6.3

Q # 10

	a	b	c	d	e	f
Freq.	25	27	28	17	15	3
% R.	78	84	88	53	47	9.4

Q #12

	a	b	c	d
Freq.	14	15	23	5
% R.	48	52	79	17

Q # 13

	a	b	c	d
Freq.	26	13	17	12
% R.	84	42	55	39

Freq. = Number of respomses
% R. = Percentage of frequency response to total number

Table A.7
Percentage of Information Workers and Teleworkers to Labor Force (Question 11)

Total Population (52)

YEAR	1990		1995		2000	
	Info W.	Tele W.	Info W.	Tele W.	Info W.	Tele W.
Stan	13.80	9.22	13.14	10.47	15.72	14.24
Max	65.00	40.00	75.00	49.00	85.00	60.00
Min	20.00	1.00	25.00	2.00	30.00	4.00
Med	42.50	20.50	50.00	25.50	57.50	32.00
AVG	42.24	11.48	50.48	17.22	59.24	25.19

Academicians (14)

	Info W.	Tele W.	Info W.	Tele W.	Info W.	Tele W.
Stan	13.67	8.60	11.77	9.78	13.12	15.36
Max	60.00	30.00	70.00	35.00	80.00	50.00
Min	20.00	1.00	25.00	2.00	30.00	4.00
AVG	45.36	9.30	52.36	13.90	58.82	21.50

Public officials (5)

	Info W.	Tele W.	Info W.	Tele W.	Info W.	Tele W.
Stan	11.79	10.53	14.34	8.81	21.21	4.50
Max	55.00	30.00	65.00	35.00	75.00	35.00
Min	30.00	5.00	30.00	15.00	30.00	24.00
AVG	38.33	15.67	46.67	22.67	60.00	29.67

Business Executives (33)

	Info W.	Tele W.	Info W.	Tele W.	Info W.	Tele W.
Stan	13.82	9.02	13.51	10.52	16.07	14.22
Max	65.00	40.00	75.00	49.00	85.00	60.00
Min	20.00	2.00	25.00	5.00	30.00	8.00
AVG	41.05	11.97	50.00	18.11	59.37	26.42

Table A.8
The Impact of Teleworking on the City (Questions 14-15)

Total Population (52)

Land Use — Q #14

	a	b	c	d
YEAR				
Stan	1.13	0.88	1.2	1.12
Max	5	5	5	5
Min	1	2	1	1
Med	3	3.5	3	3
AVG	3.8	4.1	3.36	2.85

Transportation System — Question #15

	a			b			c			d		
YEAR	1990	1995	2000	1990	1995	2000	1990	1995	2000	1990	1995	2000
Stan	2.85	5.63	9.39	3.34	6.38	9.26	3.5	5.93	9.96	3.66	6.61	8.96
Max	10	25	50	10	30	40	15	25	40	10	20	30
Min	0	0	0	0	0	0	0	0	0	0	0	0
Med	5	12.5	25	5	15	20	7.5	12.5	20	5	10	15
AVG	3.15	7.03	12	3.91	7.97	12.4	4.21	7.46	12.5	3.68	7.11	10.1

Academicians (14)

Land Use

	a	b	c	d
Stan	1.24	0.92	1	1.3
Max	5	5	5	5
Min	1	2	2	1
AVG	4	4.08	3.62	2.75

Transportation System

	a			b			c			d		
YEAR	1990	1995	2000	1990	1995	2000	1990	1995	2000	1990	1995	2000
Stan	1.78	3.65	6.5	1.71	3.35	6.36	2.86	5.49	10.3	3.66	7.17	8.88
Max	5	10	20	5	10	20	10	20	30	10	20	30
Min	0	0	0	0	0	0	0	0	0	0	0	0
AVG	1.55	3.45	7.33	1.73	3.82	7.08	2.73	5	9.92	2.82	5.55	8.17

Public officals (5)

Land Use

	a	b	c	d
Stan	1.2	0.75	1.17	0.75
Max	5	5	5	4
Min	2	3	2	2
AVG	3.4	4.2	3.8	2.8

Transportation System

	a			b			c			d		
YEAR	1990	1995	2000	1990	1995	2000	1990	1995	2000	1990	1995	2000
Stan	3.3	5.66	7.54	3.3	6.98	10.7	5.56	9.18	14.7	0.5	3.5	4
Max	10	15	20	10	20	30	15	25	40	3	10	12
Min	2	3	4	3	3	4	2	3	4	2	3	4
AVG	5.67	11	14.7	5.67	11	16.37		12.7	21.3	2.5	6.5	8

Business Executives (33)

Land Use

	a	b	c	d
Stan	1.05	0.88	1.24	1.09
Max	5	5	5	5
Min	1	2	1	1
AVG	3.78	4.09	3.19	2.9

Transportation System

	a			b			c			d		
YEAR	1990	1995	2000	1990	1995	2000	1990	1995	2000	1990	1995	2000
Stan	2.79	5.51	10	3.43	6.44	9.08	4.15	6.74		3.7	6.25	9.1
Max	10	25	50	10	30	40	15	30		10	20	30
Min	0	0	5	0	0	0	0	0		0	0	0
AVG	3.68	8.47	14.6	4.89	9.89	15.1	8.29	12.9		4.47	8.33	12

Table A.9
Teleactivity and Social Implications (Questions 16, 21)

| | Teleworking and Social Relations | | | | | | | Urban Pattern | | | |

Total Population (52)

Question	Q # 16							Q # 21			
	a	b	c	d	e	f	g	a	b	c	d
Freq.	36	13	12	30	17	37	52	16	40	28	42
% R.	72	26	24	60	34	74	104	34.78	86.96	60.87	91.3

Academicians (14)

	a	b	c	d	e	f	g	a	b	c	d
Freq.	6	2	4	5	2	7	14	5	10	5	13
% R.	46.15	15.38	30.77	38.46	15.38	53.85	107.7	41.67	83.33	41.67	108.3

Public Officials (5)

	a	b	c	d	e	f	g	a	b	c	d
Freq.	4	1	2	2	2	3	5	1	3	2	3
% R.	80	20	40	40	40	60	100	33.33	100	66.67	100

Business Executives (33)

	a	b	c	d	e	f	g	a	b	c	d
Freq.	26	10	6	23	13	27	33	10	27	21	26
% R.	81.25	31.25	18.75	71.88	40.63	84.38	103.1	32.26	87.1	67.74	83.87

Freq. = Number of responses
% R. = Percentage of frequency response to total number

129

Table A.10
Teleworking Impact on Social Relations (Questions 17, 18)

% Favor Teleworking Strategy   Average Distance

Total Population (52)

Q #	Q # 17			Q # 18			
	a	b	c	a	b	c	d
Stan	18.25	13.35	6.13	15.33	66.53	20.30	8.45
Max	95.00	60.00	25.00	100.00	400.00	100.00	35.00
Min	20.00	4.00	1.00	3.00	2.00	1.00	0.50
Med	57.50	32.00	13.00	51.50	201.00	50.50	17.75
AVG	70.78	20.65	8.57	17.78	30.07	13.93	14.64

Academicians (14)

	a	b	c	a	b	c	d
Stan	12.21	8.50	5.37	6.52	29.74	38.35	6.94
Max	85.00	30.00	20.00	25.00	100.00	100.00	25.00
Min	50.00	10.00	2.00	5.00	2.00	2.00	0.50
AVG	69.00	21.30	9.70	12.80	21.22	32.50	10.83

Public Officials

	a	b	c	a	b	c	d
Stan	0.00	0.00	0.00	34.90	155.31	4.15	5.75
Max	50.00	30.00	20.00	100.00	400.00	15.00	20.00
Min	50.00	30.00	20.00	3.00	10.00	5.00	3.00
AVG	50.00	30.00	20.00	31.60	89.40	8.75	12.60

Business Executives (33)

	a	b	c	a	b	c	d
Stan	19.92	14.90	6.00	9.96	37.97	6.64	8.83
Max	95.00	60.00	25.00	50.00	200.00	30.00	35.00
Min	20.00	4.00	1.00	5.00	2.00	1.00	1.00
AVG	72.27	20.04	7.69	17.16	22.59	9.40	16.35

Table A.11
Telecity and Public Policy (Question 23)

Total Population (52)

Q # 23	a	b	c	d
Stan	1.54	2.29	2.62	2.48
Max	10.00	10.00	10.00	10.00
Min	1.00	2.00	1.00	1.00
Med	5.50	6.00	5.50	5.50
AVG	9.30	7.33	4.51	7.39

Academicians (14)

	a	b	c	d
Stan	1.21	2.53	2.76	2.02
Max	10.00	10.00	10.00	10.00
Min	6.00	2.00	1.00	4.00
AVG	9.17	6.00	5.40	8.46

Public Officials (5)

	a	b	c	d
Stan	0.00	1.00	2.49	0.82
Max	10.00	5.00	7.00	9.00
Min	10.00	3.00	1.00	7.00
AVG	10.00	4.00	4.33	8.00

Business Executives (33)

	a	b	c	d
Stan	1.71	1.86	2.51	2.60
Max	10.00	10.00	9.00	10.00
Min	1.00	3.00	1.00	1.00
AVG	9.29	7.97	4.21	6.87

a = Standardization
b = Deregulation
c = Mix land Uses
d = Public Investment

Bibliography

Abel, Elie. 1985. "International Communication: A New Order?" In
Everett M. Rogers and Francis Balle, eds., *The Media Revolution
in the United States and Western Europe*. Norwood, N.J.: Ablex.

Abler, Ronald. 1977. "The Telephone and the Evolution of American
Metropolitan System." In Ithiel de Sola Pool, ed., *The Social
Impact of the Telephone*. Boston, Mass.: MIT Press.

Abu-Lughod, Janet, and Richard Hay, eds. 1977. *Third World Urbanization*. Chicago: Maaroufa Press.

Adams, John. 1970. "Residential Structure of Midwestern Cities." *Annals
of the Association of American Geographers* 60: 37-62.

Agnew, J., J. Mercer, and D. Sopher, eds. 1984. *The City in Cultural
Context*. Boston: Allen & Unwin.

Alexander, Christopher. 1965. "The City Is Not a Tree." *Architectural
Forum* 122, nos. 1/2 (April/May).

Alexander, C., S. Ishishikawa, and M. Silverstein. 1975. *The Pattern
Language: Towns, Buildings, Construction*. New York: Oxford
University Press.

Allison, Graham T. 1971. *Essence of Decision: Explaining the Cuban
Missile Crisis*. Boston: Little, Brown and Company.

Alonso, William. 1964. *Location and Land Use*. Cambridge, Mass.:
Harvard University Press.

_____. 1978. "A Theory of Movement." In N. M. Hansen, ed., *Human
Settlement Systems*. Cambridge, Mass.: Ballinger.

Amin, Samir. 1974. *Accumulation on a World Scale: A Critique of the Theory of Underdevelopment.* New York: Monthly Review Press.
_____. 1976. *Unequal Development: An Essay on the Social Transformation of Peripheral Capitalism.* New York: Monthly Review Press.
Appleyard, Donald. 1979. "The Environment as a Social Symbol: Within a Theory of Environmental Action and Perception." *APA Journal* (April): 143-153.
_____. 1981. *Livable Streets.* Berkeley: University of California Press.
Aronson, Sidney H. 1971. "The Sociology of the Telephone." *International Journal of Comparative Sociology* 12 (September): 153-167.
_____. 1977. "Bell's Electrical Toy: What's the Use? The Sociology of Early Telephone Usage." In Ithiel de Sola Pool, ed., *The Social Impact of the Telephone*, 15-39. Boston, Mass.: MIT Press.
Arrow, Kenneth J. 1963. *Social Choice and Individual Values.* New Haven, Conn.: Yale University Press.
Ayres, R. U. 1969. *Technological Forecasting and Long Range Planning.* New York: McGraw-Hill.
Bacon, Francis. 1870. "Advancement of Learning." In James Spedding, Robert Ellis, and Douglas Heath, eds., *The Work of Francis Bacon.* London: Longmans & Co.
_____. 1885. "Atlantis." In Henry Morley, ed., *Ideal Commonwealths.* New York: E. P. Dutton & Co.
Baer, Walter S. 1985. "Information Technologies in the Home." In Bruce R. Guile, ed., *Information Technologies and Social Transformation.* Washington, D.C.: National Academy Press.
Baier, Kurt. 1965. *The Moral Point of View: A Rational Basis of Ethics.* New York: Random House.
Bair, K., and N. Rescher, eds. 1969. *Technology and Value Change: The Impact of Technological Change on American Values.* New York: Free Press.
Ball, D. 1986. "Toward a Sociology of Telephones and Telephoners." In Marcello Truzzi, ed., *Sociology and Everyday Life.* Englewood Cliffs, N.J.: Prentice-Hall.
Banfield, Edward C. 1970. *The Unheavenly City.* Boston: Little, Brown and Company.
Baran, Barbara. 1985. "Office Automation and Women's Work: The Technological Transformation of the Insurance Industry." In M. Castells, ed., *High Techology, Space, and Society.* Beverly Hills, Calif.: Sage.
Barber, Bernard. 1962. *Science and the Social Order.* New York: Collier Books.

Barbour, Ian G. 1980. *Technology, Environment, and Human Values.* New York: Praeger Publishers.

Beer, Stafford. 1967. *Cybernetics and Management*, 3d ed. New York: John Wiley & Sons.

Belitsos, Byron, and Jay Misra. 1986. *Business Telematics: Corporate Networks for the Information Age.* New York: Dow Jones-Irwin.

Bell, Daniel. 1967. *The End of Ideology.* New York: Free Press.

――――. 1973. *The Coming Post-Industrial Society.* New York: Basic Books.

Benevolo, Leonardo. 1971. *The Origins of Modern Town Planning.* Cambridge, Mass.: MIT Press.

Beniger, James. 1986. *The Control Revolution: Technological and Economic Origins of Information Society.* Boston: Harvard University Press.

Beres, L., and H. Targ, eds. 1975. *Planning Alternative World Futures: Values, Methods, and Models.* New York: Praeger Publishers.

Berger, Peter L. 1984. *Pyramids of Sacrifice: Political Ethics and Social Change.* Garden City, N.Y.: Random House.

Berger, P. L., and T. Luckmann. 1967. *The Social Construction of Reality.* Garden City, N.Y.: Anchor Books, Doubleday & Co.

Bernal, J. D. 1939. *The Social Function of Science.* New York: Macmillan Co.

Boguslaw, Robert. 1965. *The New Utopians: A Study of System Design and Social Change.* London: Prentice-Hall.

――――. 1972. "Technology and Humanism." In Charles Thrall and Jerald Starr, eds., *Technology, Power, and Social Change.* Lexington, Mass.: Lexington Books.

Boucher, W. I. 1977. "Introduction." In W. I. Boucher, ed., *The Study of the Future: An Agenda for Research.* Washington, D.C.: National Science Foundation.

Boulding, Kenneth E. 1969. *The Image.* Ann Arbor: University of Michigan Press.

Bowes, John E. 1981. "Japan's Approach to an Information Society: Critical Perspective." In Wilhoit and Bock, eds., *Mass Communication Review Year Book*, vol. 2. Beverly Hills, Calif.: Sage.

Briggs, R. 1973. "Urban Cognitive Distance." In R. Downs and D. Stea, eds., *Image and Environment.* Chicago: Aldine.

Brittan, S. 1975. *Participation Without Politics.* London: Institute of Economic Affairs.

Brotchie, J. F. 1984. "Technological Change and Urban Form." *Environment and Planning A* 16: 583-596.

Brotchie, J., P. Newton, P. Hall and P. Nijkamp, eds. 1985. *The Future of Urban Form.* London: Croom Helm.

Brown, Lester. 1972. *World Without Borders*. New York: Random House.

Brzezinski, Zbigniew. 1970. *Between Two Ages: America's Role in the Technetronic Age*. New York: Viking Press.

Calvino, Italo. 1974. *Invisible Cities*, trans. William Weaver. New York: Harcourt Brace Jovanovich.

Campbell, Jeremy. 1982. *Grammatical Man*. London: Penguin Books.

Caruso, D., and R. Palm. 1973. "Social Space and Social Place." *Professional Geographer* 25: 221-225.

Castells, Manuel. 1976. "The Service Economy and Postindustrial Society: A Sociological Critique." *International Journal of Health Services* 6, no. 4.

_____. 1977. *The Urban Question: A Marxist Approach*. Cambridge, Mass.: MIT Press.

_____. 1979. *City, Class and Power*. New York: St. Martin's Press.

_____. 1983a. "Crisis, Planning, and the Quality of Life: Managing the New Historical Relationship Between Space and Society." *Environment and Planning D: Space and Society* 1: 3-21.

_____. 1983b. *The City and the Grassroots: A Cross-Cultural Theory of Urban Social Movement*. Berkeley: University of California Press.

_____. 1984. "Toward the Information City?" Working Paper No. 430. Berkeley: University of California.

_____, ed. 1985. *High Technology, Space, and Society*. Beverly Hills, Calif.: Sage Publications.

Cetron, Marvin J. 1969. *Technological Forecasting: A Practical Approach*. New York: Gordon and Breach, Science Publishers.

Chamberlin, E. H. 1933. *The Theory of Monopolistic Competition: A Reorientation of the Theory of Value*. Cambridge, Mass.: Harvard University Press.

Cherry, Colin. 1977. "The Telephone System: Creator of Mobility and Social Change." In Ithiel de Sola Pool, ed., *The Social Impact of the Telephone*. Boston, Mass.: MIT Press.

Chilcote, Ronald H. 1981. *Theories of Comparative Politics: The Search for a Paradigm*. Boulder, Colo.: Westview Press.

Christaller, Walter. 1966 (orig. 1933). *Central Places in Southern Germany*, trans. C. W. Baskin. Englewood Cliffs, N.J.: Prentice-Hall.

Churchman, C. West. 1971. *The Design of Inquiring Systems: Basic Concepts of Systems and Organization*. New York: Basic Books.

Clark, Colin. 1941. *The Conditions of Economic Progress*. London: Macmillan Press.

Clark, Robin. 1985. *Science and Technology in the World Development*. Oxford: Oxford University Press/Unesco.

Clawson, Marion. 1971. *Suburban Land Conversion in the United States: An Economic and Governmental Process*. Baltimore: Johns Hopkins University Press.

Cole, K., J. Cameron, and C. Edward. 1983. *Why Economists Disagree: The Political Economy of Economics*. London: Longman.

Compaine, Benjamin M., ed. 1984. *Understanding New Media: Trends and Issues in Electronic Distribution of Information*. Cambridge, Mass.: Ballinger Publishers.

Corbusier, Le. 1971 (orig. 1924). *The City of Tomorrow*, trans. Frederic Etchells. Cambridge, Mass.: MIT Press.

Cornish, Edward. 1977. *The Study of the Future*. Washington, D.C.: World Future Society.

Crane, David. 1960. "The City Symbolic." *Journal of the American Institute of Planners* 26 (November).

Cross, Thomas B., and Marjorie Raizman. 1986. *Telecommuting: The Future of Technology of Work*. Homewood, Ill.: Dow Jones-Irwin.

Dear, Michael. 1986. "Postmodern Planning." *Environment and Planning D: Society and Space* 4.

Dear, M., and A. J. Scott, eds. 1981 *Urbanization and Urban Planning in Capitalist Society*. New York: Methuen.

Dertouzas, M., and J. Moses, eds. 1981 *The Computer Age: A Twenty Year View*. Cambridge, Mass.: MIT Press.

Descartes, René. 1951. *A Discourse on Method*, trans. John Veitch. New York: Everyman's Library.

Deutsch, Karl W. 1961. "On Social Communication and the Metropolis." In L. Rodwin, ed., *The Future Metropolis*. New York: George Braziller.

Dizard, Wilson P. 1982. *The Coming Information Age: An Overview of Technology, Economics, and Politics*. New York: Longman.

Dordick, Herbert, and Fredrick Williams. 1986. *Innovative Management Using Telecommunications: A Guide to Opportunities, Strategies, and Applications*. New York: John Wiley & Sons.

Dordick, H., H. Bradley, B. Names, and T. H. Martin. 1979. "Network Information Services: The Emergence of an Industry." *Telecommunication* (September): 217-234.

Dos Santos, Theotonio. 1970. "The Structure of Dependency." *American Economic Review* 60 (May): 231-236.

Downs, Anthony. 1976. *Urban Problems and Prospects*, 2d ed. Chicago: Rand McNally.

Doxiadis, C. A., and R. Dubos. 1975. *Anthropopolis: City for Human Development*. New York: Norton.

Dubos, R. 1972. *A God Within*. New York: Charles Scribner and Sons.

Duhl, Leonard J., ed. 1963. *The Urban Condition: People and Policy in the Metropolis.* New York: Simon and Schuster.

Dutton, William H., Jay G. Blumler, and Kenneth L. Kraemer, eds. 1988. *Wired Cities: Shaping the Future of Communications.* Boston, Mass.: G. K. Hall & Co.

Dyckman, John. 1961. "The Changing Uses of the City." In L. Rodwin, ed., *The Future Metropolis.* New York: George Braziller.

Elias, C. E., J. Gillies, and S. Riemer, eds. 1964. *Metropolis: Values in Conflict.* Belmont, Calif.: Wadsworth Publishing Co.

Elliott, John E. 1985. *Comparative Economic Systems*, 2d ed. Belmont, Calif.: Wadsworth Publication Co.

Ellul, Jacques. 1967. *The Technological Society.* New York: Alfred A. Knopf.

El-Sawy, Omar. 1985. *The Impact of Information Technology on the Strategic Redefinition of Organizational Domains.* A paper submitted to the Business Policy and Planning Division of the 45th Annual Meeting of the Academy of Management, San Diego, Calif.

El-Shishini, Nadia. 1983. "Technology Transfer and Technological Dependency in Developing Countries." *Journal of Social Science* (Kuwait) 11, no. 4.

Enzer, S., and R. Wurgburger. 1982. *LA. 200 + 20: Some Alternative Futures for Los Angeles 2001.* Los Angeles: University of Southern California, Center for Futures Research.

Erlander, S. 1977. "Accessibility, Entropy, and the Distribution and Assignment of Traffic." *Transportation Research* 11: 149-153.

Evans, Alan. 1973. *The Economics of Residential Location.* New York: St. Martin's Press.

Fainstein, Norman, and Susan Fainstein, eds. 1982. *Urban Policy under Capitalism.* Beverly Hills, Calif.: Sage.

Faludi, Andreas. 1973. *Planning Theory.* New York: Pergamon Press.

Farely, J., and N. J. Glickman. 1986. "R&D as an Economic Development Strategy: The Microelectronic and Computer Technology Corporation Comes to Austin, Texas." *Journal of the American Planning Association* 52: 507-413.

Fathy, Hasan. 1973. "Constancy, Transposition, and Change in the Arab City." In C. L. Brown, ed., *From Madena to Metropolis.* Princeton, N.J.: Drawn Press.

Fathy, Hisham. 1987. "Ethics and Political Thought—A Search in Religion and Ideology." In E. Alexander, ed., *Proceedings of the 1987 Conference on Planning and Design in Urban and Regional Planning.* International Congress on Planning and Design Theory, Boston, Mass. New York: American Society of Mechanical Engineers.

Fathy, Tarik. 1987. "New Information Technologies' Impact on City Form in Three Perspectives." In E. Alexander, ed., *Proceedings of the 1987 Conference on Planning and Design in Urban and Regional Planning*. International Congress on Planning and Design Theory, Boston, Mass. New York: American Society of Mechanical Engineers.

Fathy, T., L. Wingo, and O. El-Sawy. 1986. *The High-Touch Telecity: Kawasaki City of the Future*. Unpublished Report. Kawasaki, Japan: International Concept Design Competition for an Information City.

Faulhaber, G., Eli Noam, and Roberta Tasly, eds. 1986. *Services in Transition: The Impact of Information Technology on the Service Sector*. Cambridge, Mass.: Ballinger.

Fine, B. 1975. *Marx's Capital*. London: Macmillan.

Fischer, Claude S. 1985. "Studying Technology and Social Life." In M. Castells, ed., *High Technology, Space, and Society*. Beverly Hills, Calif.: Sage.

Fischer, Frank. 1980. *Politics, Values, and Public Policy*. Boulder, Colo.: Westview Press.

Fleisher, Aaron. 1960. "The Influence of Technology on Urban Forms." In L. Rodwin, ed., *The Future Metropolis*. New York: George Braziller.

Forester, John. 1980. "Critical Theory and Planning Practice." *Journal of the American Planning Association* 46.

Forester, Thomas P., ed. 1985. *The Microelectronics Revolution: The Complete Guide to New Technology and Its Impact on Society*. Cambridge, Mass.: MIT Press.

Frank, André Gunder. 1980. *Crisis in the World Economy*. New York: Holmes & Meier.

Friedman, Milton. 1953. *Essays in Positive Economics*. Chicago: University of Chicago Press.

Friedmann, John. 1978. "Innovation, Flexible Response, and Social Learning: A Problem in the Theory of Meta-Planning." In R. Burchell and G. Sternleib, eds., *Planning Theory in the 1980s*. New Brunswick, N.J.: Center for Urban Policy Research, Rutgers University.

Fuchs, Victor. 1968. *The Service Economy*. New York: Columbia University Press.

Galbraith, John Kenneth. 1958. *The Affluent Society*. Cambridge, Mass.: Riverside Press.

———. 1967. *The New Industrial State*. Boston: Houghton Mifflin.

Geertz, C. 1973. *The Interpretation of Cultures: Selected Essays*. New York: Basic Books.

Gendron, B. 1977. *Technology and Human Condition.* New York: St. Martin's Press.

Gershuny, Jonathan. 1978. *After Industrial Society?: The Emerging Self-Service Economy.* Atlantic Highlands, N.J.: Humanities Press.

———. 1983. *Social Innovation and the Division of Labor.* New York: Oxford University Press.

Gibson, D. V., and E. M. Rogers. 1988. "The MCC Comes to Texas." In F. Williams, ed., *Measuring the Information Society: The Texas Studies.* Newbury Park, Calif.: Sage.

Gibson, E. 1970. "Understanding the Subjective Meaning of Places." In D. Ley and M. Samuels, eds., *Humanistic Geography.* Chicago: Maaroufa.

Giddens, A. 1981. *A Contemporary Critique of Historical Materialism.* Berkeley: University of California Press.

Glasmeier, Amy. 1985. "Innovative Manufacturing Industries: Spatial Incidence in the United States." In M. Castells, ed., *High Technology, Space, and Society.* Beverly Hills, Calif.: Sage.

Glasmeier, Amy, A. Markusen, and P. Hall. 1983. *Defining High-Tech.* Institute of Urban and Regional Development Working Paper No. 407. Berkeley: University of California.

Goffman, E. 1959. *The Presentation of Self in Everyday Life.* Garden City, N.Y.: Doubleday.

———. 1963. *Behavior in Public Spaces: Notes on the Social Organization of Gatherings.* New York: Free Press.

———. 1973. *Frame Analysis: An Essay on the Organization of Experience.* New York: Harper & Row.

Golany, Gideon, ed. 1976. *Innovations for Future Cities.* New York: Praeger Publishers.

Goldthrope, J. E. 1984. *The Sociology of the Third World: Disparity and Development.* Cambridge: Cambridge University Press.

Goodin, Robert E. 1982. *Political Theory and Public Policy.* Chicago: University of Chicago Press.

Gordon, Theodore J. 1985. "Computer and Business." In Bruce R. Guile, ed., *Information Technologies and Social Transformation.* Washington, D.C.: National Academy Press.

Gorz, André. 1968. *Strategy for Labor.* Boston: Beacon Press.

Gottdiener, Mark. 1985. *The Social Production of Urban Space.* Austin: University of Texas Press.

Gottmann, Jean. 1961. *Megalopolis.* New York: Twentieth Century Fund.

———. 1977. "Megalopolis and Antipolis: The Telephone and Structure of the City." In Ithiel de Sola Pool, ed., *The Social Impact of the Telephone.* Boston, Mass.: MIT Press.

Gouldner, A. W. 1976. *The Dialectic of Ideology and Technology: The Origins, Grammar and Future of Ideology.* London: Macmillan.
_____. 1979. *The Future of Intellectuals and the Rise of the New Class.* New York: Seabury Press, Continuum.
Greene, D. L. 1980. "Recent Trends in Urban Spatial Structure." *Growth and Change* (May): 29-40.
Greenhut, Melvin. 1971. *A Theory of the Firm in Economic Space.* Austin, Tex.: Lone Star Publishers.
Guile, Bruce, ed. 1985. *Information Technologies and Social Transformation.* Washington, D.C.: National Academy Press.
Gunnel, John G. 1982. "The Technocratic Image and the Theory of Technology." *Technology and Culture* 23: 392-416.
Haberer, Joseph. 1969. *Politics and the Community of Science.* New York: Van Nostrand Reinhold.
Habermas, Jürgen. 1970. *Toward a Rational Society.* Boston: Beacon Press.
_____. 1973. *Theory and Practice.* Boston: Beacon Press.
Hall, Peter. 1980. *Great Planning Disasters.* Berkeley: University of California Press.
_____. 1984. *The World Cities.* New York: St. Martin's Press.
_____. 1985. "Technology, Space, and Society in Contemporary Britain." In M. Castells, ed., *High Technology, Space, and Society.* Beverly Hills, Calif.: Sage.
Hall, Peter, and Ann Markusen, eds. 1985. *Silicon Landscapes.* London: Allen and Unwin.
Hartshorn, T. 1980. *Interpreting the City: An Urban Geography.* New York: John Wiley & Sons.
Harvey, David. 1976. "Labor, Capital and Class Struggle around the Built Environment." *Politics and Society* 6: 265-295.
Hawks, Nigel. 1971. *The Computer Revolution.* New York: E. P. Dutton.
Helmer, Olaf. 1966. *Social Technology.* New York: Basic Books.
Henderson, J. 1975. "Congestion and Optimum City Size." *Journal of Urban Economics* 2.
Hirschhorn, Larry. 1974. *Towards a Political Economy of the Service Society.* Berkeley, Calif.: Institute of Urban and Regional Develment Working Paper 229.
_____. 1985. "Information Technology and the New Service Game." In M. Castells, ed., *High Technology, Space, and Society.* Beverly Hills, Calif.: Sage.
Hoffmann, Erik, and Robbin F. Laird. 1985. *Technocratic Socialism: The Soviet Union in the Advanced Industrial Era.* Durham, N.C.: Duke University Press.

Hornik, Robert. 1980. "Communication as Complement in Development." *Journal of Communication* 30: 10-24.

Hough, Granville W. 1975. *Technology Diffusion: Federal Programs and Procedures.* Mt. Airy, Md.: Lomond Books.

Howard, Ebenezer. 1965 (orig. 1898). *Garden Cities of Tomorrow.* Cambridge, Mass.: MIT Press.

Hutchinson, B. G. 1976. "Land Use-Transport Models in Regional Development Planning." *Socio-Economic Planning Sciences* 10: 47-55.

Ihde, Don. 1986. *Consequences of Phenomenology.* Albany: State University of New York.

Ingelstam, L. 1977. "Basic Problems in Planning." In Jennergren et al., eds., *Trends in Planning.* London: John Wiley & Sons.

Ito, Youichi. 1981. "The Johoka Shakai: Approach to the Study of Communications in Japan." *Keio Communication Review* 2: 13-40.

Jantsch, Erich. 1972. *Technological Planning and Social Futures.* New York: John Wiley & Sons.

Kahn, Herman. 1982. *The Coming Boom: Economic, Political, Social.* New York: Simon and Schuster.

Kahn, H., and A. Wiener. 1967. *The Year 2000.* New York: Macmillan.

Kain, J. F. 1988. "Choosing the Wrong Technology: Or How to Spend Billions and Reduce Transit Use." *Journal of Advanced Transportation* 21: 197-213.

Katzman, Nathan. 1974. "The Impact of Communication Technology: Some Theoretical Premises and Their Implications." *Ekistics* 225: 125-130.

Keen, Peter G. W. 1986. *Competing in Time: Using Telecommunications for Competitive Advantage.* Boston, Mass.: Ballinger.

Keller, Suzanne. 1977. "The Telephone in New (and Old) Communities." In Ithiel de Sola Pool, ed., *The Social Impact of the Telephone.* Boston, Mass.: MIT Press.

Kerr, Clark. 1983. *The Future of Industrial Societies.* Cambridge, Mass.: Harvard University Press.

Keynes, J. M. 1936. *The General Theory of Employment, Interest and Money.* London: Macmillan.

Khalaaf, Hani A. 1986. *Futurism and the Egyptian Society.* Kitab Alhilal April, Cairo: Dar Alhilal (in Arabic).

King, Alexander. 1975. "The Future as a Discipline and the Future of the Disciplines." In Symposium No. 36, *The Future as an Academic Discipline.* London: Ciba Foundation.

Kling, Christian. 1976. *Urban Transportation.* New York: Vantage Press.

Kranzberg, Melvin. 1967. "The Unity of Science-Technology." *American Scientist* 55: 48-66.

_____. 1985. "The Information Age: Evolution or Revolution." In Bruce R. Guile, ed., *Information Technologies and Social Transformation*. Washington, D.C.: National Academy Press.

Kuhn, Thomas. 1970. *The Structure of Scientific Revolution*. Chicago: University of Chicago Press.

Kurzweil, Edith. 1980. *The Age of Structuralism: Lévi-Strauss to Foucault*. New York: Columbia University Press.

Lake, Robert, ed. 1983. *Readings in Urban Analysis: Perspectives on Urban Form and Structure*. New Brunswick, N.J.: Center for Urban Policy Research, Rutgers University.

Lasswell, Harold. 1947. *The Analysis of Political Behavior*. New York: Oxford University Press.

Lenin, V. I. 1977. "Imperialism: The Highest Stage of Capitalism." In Janet Abu-Lughod and Richard Hay, eds., *Third World Urbanization*. Chicago: Maaroufa Press.

Lerman, S. R. 1976. "Location, Housing, Automobile Ownership, and Mode to Work: A Joint Choice Model." *Transportation Research Record* 610: 6-11.

Lerner, D. 1958. *The Passing of Traditional Society: Modernizing the Middle East*. Glencoe, Ill.: Free Press.

LeVine, James B. 1984. *The Two Science Communities and Coastal Wetlands Policy*. Doctoral Dissertation, University of Southern California, School of Urban and Regional Planning, Los Angeles.

Lévi-Strauss, C. 1978. *Myth and Meaning*. New York: Schocken.

Lewis, Russel. 1973. *The New Service Society*. London: Longman.

Ley, David. 1983. *A Social Geography of the City*. New York: Harper & Row Publishers.

Lindblom, Charles. 1977. *Politics and Markets*. New York: Basic Books.

Linstone, H., and W. Simmons, eds. 1977. *Futures Research: New Directions*. Reading, Mass.: Addison-Wesley Publishers.

Linstone, H., and M. Turoff, eds. 1975. *The Delphi Method: Techniques and Applications*. Reading, Mass.: Addison-Wesley Publishers.

Lösch, August. 1954 (orig. 1939). *The Economics of Location*, trans. W. Waglom and W. Stolper. New Haven, Conn.: Yale University Press.

Lynch, Kevin. 1960. *The Image of the City*. Cambridge, Mass.: MIT Press.

_____. 1961. "The Pattern of the Metropolis." In L. Rodwin, ed., *The Future Metropolis*. New York: George Braziller.

_____. 1971. *Site Planning*, 2d ed. Cambridge, Mass.: MIT Press.

_____. 1972. *What Time Is This Place?* Cambridge, Mass.: MIT Press.

_____. 1984. *Good City Form*. Cambridge, Mass.: MIT Press.

Lyon, David. 1986. *The Silicon Society: How Will Information Technology Change Our Lives?* Grand Rapids, Mich.: W. B. Eerdmans.

McAnany, Emile G. 1984. "The Diffusion of Innovation: Why Does It Endure?" *Critical Studies in Mass Communication* 1, no. 4: 439-442.

McCarthy, Thomas. 1978. *The Critical Theory of Jürgen Habermas.* Cambridge, Mass.: MIT Press.

Machlup, Fritz. 1962. *The Production and Distribution of Knowledge in the United States.* Princeton, N.J.: Princeton University Press.

McLuhan, Marshall. 1964. *Understanding Media: The Extension of Man.* New York: McGraw-Hill.

Madden, J. 1981. "Why Women Work Closer to Home." *Urban Studies* 18: 181-194.

Malecki, Edward. 1983. "Technology and Regional Development: A Survey." *International Regional Science Review* 8: 12-45.

———. 1984. "High Technology and Local Economic Development." *Journal of the American Planning Association* 50, no. 3: 297-310.

Mallet, Serge. 1963. *La Nouvelle Classe Ouvrière.* Paris: Editions du Seuil.

Mandelbaum, S. 1972. *Community and Communication.* New York: W. W. Norton & Co.

Mannheim, Karl. 1936 (orig. 1929). *Ideology and Utopia.* New York: Harcourt, Brace & World.

Marchand, Donald, and Forest Horton. 1986. *Infotrends: Profiting from Your Information Resources.* New York: John Wiley & Sons.

Marcuse, Herbert. 1964. *One-Dimensional Man: Studies in the Ideology of Advanced Industrial Society.* Boston: Beacon Press.

Marin, James. 1978. *The Wired Society.* Englewood Cliffs, N.J.: Prentice-Hall.

———. 1981. *The Telematic Society: A Challenge for Tomorrow.* Englewood Cliffs, N.J.: Prentice-Hall.

Markusen, Ann, and Robin Bolch. 1985. "Defensive Cities: Military Spending, High Technology, and Human Settlements." In M. Castells, ed., *High Technology, Space, and Society.* Beverly Hills, Calif.: Sage.

Markusen, Ann, P. Hall, and A. Glasmeier. 1986. *High Tech America: The What, How, Where, and Why of the Sunrise Industries.* Boston: Allen & Unwin.

Marshall, A. 1947. *Principles of Economics.* London: Macmillan.

Marx, Karl. 1970 (orig. 1867). *Capital, Volume One and Two.* London: Lawrence and Wishart.

Marx, Karl, and F. Engels. 1977. "The City, the Division of Labor, and

the Emergence of Capitalism." In Janet Abu-Lughod and Richard
Hay, eds., *Third World Urbanization*. Chicago: Maaroufa Press.

Mayer, Martin. 1985. "The Videotext Revolution." In Tom Forester,
ed., *The Information Technology Revolution*. Cambridge, Mass.:
MIT Press.

Mayo, John. 1985. "The Evolution of Information Technologies."
In Bruce R. Guile, ed., *Information Technologies and Social Transformation*. Washington, D.C.: National Academy Press.

Meier, Richard. 1962. *A Communications Theory of Urban Growth*.
Cambridge, Mass.: MIT Press.

Melman, S., et al. 1972. "Symposium on Technology and Authority." In
Charles Thrall and Jerald Starr, eds. *Technology, Power, and Social
Change*. Lexington, Mass.: Lexington Books.

Merton, Robert K. 1957. "Priorities in Scientific Discovery." *American
Sociological Review* 22: 635-659.

Mesthene, Emmanuel. 1970. *Technological Change*. Cambridge, Mass.:
Harvard University Press.

Meyrowitz, J. 1985. *No Sense of Place: The Impact of Electronic Media
on Social Behavior*. New York: Oxford University Press.

Michael, Donald. 1977. "Planning's Challenge to the Systems Approach."
In H. Linstone and W. Simmonds, eds., *Futures Research: New
Directions*. Reading, Mass.: Addison-Wesley Publishers.

Miller, D. K. 1983. "Theory, Paradigms, and Planning." In J. R. Blau,
M. La Gory, and J. S. Pipkin, eds., *Professionals and Urban
Form*. Albany: State University of New York Press.

Miller, R., and M. Cote. 1985. "Growing the Next Silicon Valley."
Harvard Business Review 4: 114-123.

Mitroff, I., and M. Turoff. 1975. "Philosophical and Methodological
Foundations of Delphi." In Harold Linstone and Murray Turoff,
eds., *The Delphi Method: Techniques and Applications*. Reading,
Mass.: Addison-Wesley Publishers.

Moore, Wilbert E., ed. 1972. *Technology and Social Change*. Chicago:
Quadrangle Books.

More, Thomas. 1965. *Utopia*. Harmondsworth, Middlesex, England:
Penguin.

Morison, Elting E. 1966. *Men, Machines, and Modern Times*. Cambridge, Mass.: MIT Press.

Morris, A.E.J. 1972. *History of Urban Form: Prehistory to the Renaissance*. London: Routledge and Kegan Paul.

Morris, David, and Karl Hess. 1975. *Neighborhood Power: The New
Localism*. Boston: Beacon Press.

Mosco, Vincent. 1982. *Pushbutton Fantasies: Critical Perspectives on
Videotext and Information Technology*. New York: Ablex.

Moss, M. 1986. "Telecommunications and the Future of Cities." *Land Development Studies* 3: 33-44.

Mueller, Dennis C. 1979. *Public Choice*. Cambridge: Cambridge University Press.

Mumford, Lewis. 1961. *The City in History*. New York: Harcourt Brace Jovanovich.

_____. 1963a. *The Highway and the City*. New York: Harcourt Brace Jovanovich.

_____. 1963b. *Technics and Civilization*. New York: Harcourt Brace Jovanovich.

_____. 1970. *The Myth of the Machine*. New York: Harcourt Brace Jovanovich.

_____. 1972. "Two Views on Technology and Man." In Charles Thrall and Jerald Starr, eds., *Technology, Power, and Social Change*. Lexington, Mass.: Lexington Books.

Muth, R. F. 1969. *Cities and Housing*. Chicago: University of Chicago Press.

Naisbitt, John. 1982. *Megatrends*. New York: Warner Books.

Nanus, Burt. 1982. *Developing Strategies for the Information Society*. Los Angeles: University of Southern California Center for Futures Research.

Newman, Oscar. 1972. *Defensible Space*. New York: Macmillan.

Nicol, Lionel. 1985. "Communication Technology: Economic and Spatial Impacts." In M. Castells, ed., *High Technology, Space, and Society*. Beverly Hills, Calif.: Sage.

Nilles, Jack. 1984. *Managing Teleworking*. Los Angeles: University of Southern California Center for Futures Research.

_____. 1985. "Teleworking from Home." In Tom Forester, ed., *The Information Technology Revolution*. Cambridge, Mass.: MIT Press.

Ogburn, William F. 1972. "Can Science Bring Us Happiness?" In W. Moore, ed., *Technology and Social Change*. Chicago: Quadrangle Books.

Olson, Mancur. 1965. *The Logic of Collective Action*. Cambridge, Mass.: Harvard University Press.

Organization for Economic Cooperation and Development (OECD). 1983. *Telecommunication: Pressures and Policies for Change*. Paris: OECD.

_____. 1985. *The Semi-Conductor Industry: Trade Related Issues*. Paris: OECD.

Owen, Wilfred. 1972. *The Accessible City*. Washington, D.C.: The Brookings Institution.

Palm, R. I. 1973. "The Telephone and the Organization of Urban Space." *Proceedings of the Association of American Geographers* 5: 207-210.

Parson, Talcott. 1961. *The Social System.* Glencoe, Ill.: Free Press.

Pederson, E. O. 1980. *Transportation in Cities.* New York: Pergamon Press.

Perloff, Harvey S. 1980. *Planning the Post-Industrial City.* Washington, D.C.: Planners Press (APA).

Perry, Clarence. 1929. "The Neighborhood Unit." In *The Regional Plan of New York and Its Environs,* Vol. 7. New York: Regional Plan Association.

Piaget, Jean. 1970. *Structuralism.* New York: Harper & Row.

Pool, Ithiel de Sola, ed. 1977. *The Social Impact of the Telephone.* Cambridge, Mass.: MIT Press.

———. 1983a. *Technologies of Freedom.* Cambridge, Mass.: Harvard University Press.

———. 1983b. "Tracking the Flow of Information." *Science* 221: 609-613.

Popper, Karl R. 1974 (orig. 1945). *The Open Society and Its Enemies,* 2 vols. London: Routledge and Kegan Paul.

Porat, Uri Mark. 1978. "Global Implication of Information Society." *Journal of Communication* 28.

Porter, Michael E. 1985. *Competitive Advantage: Creating and Sustaining Superior Performance.* New York: Free Press.

Pred, A. 1977. *City Systems in Advanced Economies.* London: Hutchinson.

Price, Derek J. de Solla. 1961. *Science Since Babylon.* New Haven, Conn.: Yale University Press.

Raban, J. 1974. *The Soft City.* London: Collins.

Rapoport, Amos. 1969. *House Form and Culture.* Foundations of Cultural Geography Series. Englewood Cliffs, N.J.: Prentice-Hall.

———. 1977. *Human Aspects of Urban Form.* New York: Pergamon.

———. 1984. "Culture and the Urban Order." In John Agnew et al., eds., *The City in Cultural Context.* Boston: Allen & Unwin.

Relph, E. C. 1976. *Place and Placelessness.* London: Pion.

Richardson, Harry. 1978. *Urban Economics.* Hinsdale, Ill.: Dryden Press.

Richta, Radovan. 1967. *Civilization at the Crossroads: Social and Human Implications of the Scientific and Technological Revolution.* White Plains, N.Y.: International Arts and Science Press.

Rittel, H., and W. Webber. 1973. "Dilemmas in General Theory of Planning." *Policy Science* 4: 155-169.

Robinson, J. 1933. *The Economics of Imperfect Competition.* London: Macmillan.

Rodwin, Loyd, ed. 1961. *The Future Metropolis.* New York: George Braziller.

Rogers, Everett M., ed. 1976. *Communication and Development: Critical Perspectives.* Beverly Hills, Calif.: Sage.
———. 1983. *Diffusion of Innovations,* 3d ed. New York: Free Press.
———. 1984. "The Emergence of Information Societies: Introduction." Paper presented at Annenberg Washington Program's Conference on Information Societies.
———. 1985. "The Diffusion of Home Computers Among Households in Silicon Valley." *Planning and Family Review* 8.
———. 1986. *Communication Technology: The New Media in Society.* New York: Free Press.
Rogers, E., and R. Burdge. 1972. *Social Change in Rural Societies.* New York: Appleton-Century-Crofts.
Rogers, Everett M., and J. Larsen, 1984. *Silicon Valley Fever: Growth of High-Technology Culture.* New York: Basic Books.
Rogers, E. M., and P. Shoemaker, 1971. *Communication of Innovation: A Cross Cultural Approach.* New York: Free Press.
Rogers, E., and T. Valente. 1988. *Technology Transfer in High Technology Industries.* Paper presented at the Second Annual IBEAR Research Conference and the Dialectics of Technology Transfer, Los Angeles.
Rogers, M., and F. Belle, eds. 1985. *The Media Revolution in America and Western Europe.* Norwood, N.J.: Ablex.
Rorvik, David M. 1971. *As Man Becomes Machine.* New York: Doubleday.
Rosenweig, R. M. 1982. *The Research Universities and Their Patrons.* Berkeley: University of California Press.
Rostow, W. W. 1960. *The Stages of Economic Growth: A Non-Communist Manifesto.* Cambridge: Cambridge University Press.
Roth, Harry B. 1986. "Regulating Satellite Dish Antennas." *Planning Advisory Service.* American Planning Association, Report No. 394.
Russell, Bertrand. 1972. "The Science to Save Us from Science." In W. Moore, ed., *Technology and Social Change.* Chicago: Quadrangle Books.
Saarinen, Eliel. 1943. *The City: Its Growth, Its Decay, Its Future.* New York: Reinhold.
Sabel, Charles. 1982. *Work and Politics.* Cambridge, Mass.: MIT Press.
Salvagio, Jerry. 1983. "Social Problems of Information Societies." *Telecommunication Policy* (September): 228-242.
Sawers, Larry, and William Tabb, eds. 1984. *Sunbelt/Snowbelt: Urban Development and Regional Restructuring.* New York: Oxford University Press.
Saxenian, Annalee. 1984. "Growth and the Restructuring of the Semiconductor Industry." In L. Sawers and W. Tabb, eds., *Sunbelt/*

Snowbelt: Urban Development and Regional Restructuring. New York: Oxford University Press.

_____. 1985. "Silicon Valley and Route 128: Regional Prototypes or Historic Exceptions?" In M. Castells, ed., *High Technology, Space, and Society.* Beverly Hills, Calif.: Sage.

Schon, Donald. 1967. *Technology and Change.* New York: Dell.

Schramm, Wilbur. 1964. *Mass Media and National Development.* Stanford, Calif.: Stanford University Press.

Schramm, W., and D. Lerner. 1976. *Communication and Change: The Last Ten Years and the Next.* Honolulu, Hawaii: East-West Center Press.

Schumpeter, J. A. 1954. *History of Economic Analysis.* Oxford: Oxford University Press.

Schwarz, B., U. Svedin, and B. Wittrock. 1982. *Methods in Futures Studies: Problems and Applications.* Boulder, Colo.: Westview Press.

Scovill, Kim Robert. 1985. *An Introduction to the Regulation of Telecommunications.* Chicago: Telephony Publishing Co.

Senn, James A. 1987. *Information Systems in Management.* Belmont, Calif.: Wadsworth Publishing Co.

Shani, M. 1974. "Futures Studies Versus Planning." *Omega* 2, no. 5: 635-645.

Sheth, Jagdish N., Jack Nilles, and M. Saghafi. 1987. *Telecommunication Outlook 1987.* Los Angeles, Calif.: University of Southern California, Center for Telecommunication Management.

Sigel, Efrem. 1983. *The Future of Videotext.* Englewood Cliffs, N.J.: Prentice-Hall.

Simlor, R. W., G. Kozmetsky, and D. V. Gibson, eds. 1988. *Technopolis: Technology and Economic Development in the Modern City State.* Boston, Mass.: Ballinger.

Simon, Herbert A. 1981. *The Sciences of the Artificial.* Cambridge, Mass.: MIT Press.

Simon, John J., ed. 1986. *From Sand to Circuits: And Other Inquiries.* Cambridge, Mass.: Harvard University Press.

Simpson, W. 1987. "Workplace Location, Residential Locations, and Urban Commuting." *Urban Studies* 24: 119-128.

Singh, Jyoti S. 1977. *A New International Economic Order.* New York: Praeger Publishers.

Smith, Adam. 1974. *Wealth of Nations.* New York: Penguin.

Smith, Anthony. 1980. *The Geopolitics of Information: How Western Culture Dominates the World.* New York: Oxford University Press.

Soja, E., R. Morales, and G. Wolff. 1983. "Urban Restructuring: An Analysis of Social and Spatial Changes in Los Angeles." *Economic Geography:* 195-230.

Solomon, Jean-Jacques. 1973. *Science and Politics,* trans. Noel Lindsay. London: Macmillan.

Southern California Association of Governments (SCAG). 1984. *Reducing Infrastructure Needs and Costs.* Los Angeles, Calif.: SCAG.

_____. 1985. *The Telecommuting Phenomenon: Overview and Evaluation.* Los Angeles, Calif.: SCAG.

Spector, A., L. Brown, and E. Malecki. 1976. "Acquaintance Circles and Communication." *Professional Geographer* 28: 267-276.

Sraffa, P. 1960. *Production of Commodities by Means of Commodities.* Cambridge: Cambridge University Press.

Stanback, Thomas M. 1979. *Understanding Service Economy.* Baltimore, Md.: Johns Hopkins University Press.

_____. 1985. "The Changing Fortunes of Metropolitan Economies." In M. Castells, ed., *High Technology, Space, and Society.* Beverly Hills, Calif.: Sage.

Stanback, T., and T. Noyelle. 1982. *Cities in Transformation.* Totowa, N.J.: Rowman and Allenheld.

Sterling, Christopher H. 1984. *International Telecommunications and Information Policy.* Washington, D.C.: Communications Press.

Stine, G. Harry. 1975. *The Third Industrial Revolution.* New York: G.P. Putman's Sons.

Stroper, Michael, and Richard Walker. 1984. "The Spatial Division of Labor: Labor and Location of Industries." In L. Sawers and W. Tabb, eds., *Sunbelt/Snowbelt: Urban Development and Regional Restructuring.* New York: Oxford University Press.

Sunkel, Oscar, and E. Fuenzalida. 1979. "Transnationalization and Its National Consequences." In Villamil, ed., *Transnational Capitalism and National Development.* Atlantic Highlands, N.J.: Humanities Press.

Sweezy, P. M. 1939. "Demand under Conditions of Oligopoly." *Journal of Political Economy.* 47.

_____. 1968. *The Theory of Capitalism Development.* New York: Monthly Review Press.

Tavel, Charles. 1975. *The Third Industrial Age: Strategy for Business Survival,* trans. Donald Caldwell. Homewood, Ill.: Dow Jones-Irwin.

Taylor, P. 1961. *Normative Discourse.* Englewood Cliffs, N.J.: Prentice-Hall.

Teich, Albert H., ed. 1981. *Technology and Man's Future,* 3d ed. New York: St. Martin's Press.

Thrall, Charles, and Jerald Starr, eds. 1972. *Technology, Power, and Social Change*. Lexington, Mass.: Lexington Books.

Thünen, J. H. Von. 1966 (orig. 1826). *Isolated State*, trans. by C. Wartenburg. London: Pergamon.

Thwaites, A., and R. Oakey, eds. 1985. *The Regional Economic Impact of Technological Change*. New York, St. Martin's Press.

Toffler, Alvin. 1970. *Future Shock*. New York: Random House.

_____. 1980. *The Third Wave*. New York: William Morrow and Company.

Toulmin, Stephen. 1977. "From Form to Function: Philosophy and History of Science in the 1950s and Now." *Daedalus* 106: 143-162.

Touraine, Alain. 1971. *The Post-Industrial Society*. New York: Random House.

Toynbee, Arnold J. 1972. "Not the Age of Atoms but of Welfare for All." In W. Moore, ed., *Technology and Social Change*. Chicago: Quadrangle Books.

Tuccille, Jerome. 1975. *Who's Afraid of 1984?* New Rochelle, N.Y.: Arlington House Publishers.

Turoff, Murray. 1975. "The Policy Delphi." In Harold Linstone and Murray Turoff, eds., *The Delphi Method: Techniques and Applications*. Reading, Mass.: Addison-Wesley.

U.S. Congress. Office of Technology Assessment. 1985. *Information Technology Research and Development: Critical Trends and Issues*. Washington, D.C.: U.S. Government Printing Office.

Veblen, T. B. 1932. *The Theory of Business Enterprise*. New York: Scribner.

_____. 1957. *The Theory of the Leisure Class*. London: Allen and Unwin.

Wachs, Martin. 1976. "Consumer Attitude Toward Transit Service: An Interpretive Review." *American Institute of Planners Journal*: 96-104.

_____. 1982. "Ethical Dilemmas in Forecasting for Public Policy." *Public Management Forum*: 562-567.

_____. 1984. "Autos, Transit, and Sprawl of Los Angeles." *Journal of the American Planning Association* 50, no. 3: 262-269.

_____, ed. 1985. *Ethics in Planning*. New Brunswick, N.J.: Center for Urban Policy Research, Rutgers University.

Wad, Atul. 1982. "Microelectronics: Implications and Strategies for the Third World." *Third World Quarterly* 4.

Walker, Richard. 1985. "Technological Determination and Determinism: Industrial Growth and Location." In M. Castells, ed., *High Technology, Space, and Society*. Beverly Hills, Calif.: Sage.

Warner, Sam Bass. 1962. *Street Car Suburbs*. Cambridge, Mass.: Harvard University Press.

Weaver, Robert C. 1963. "Major Factors in Urban Planning." In L. Duhl, ed., *The Urban Condition: People and Policy in the Metropolis*. New York: Simon and Schuster.

Webber, Melvin. 1963a. "Order in Diversity." In L. Wingo, ed., *Cities and Space*. Baltimore, Md.: Johns Hopkins University Press.

_____. 1963b. "The Prospects for Policy Planning." In L. Duhl, ed., *The Urban Condition: People and Policy in the Metropolis*. New York: Simon and Schuster.

_____. 1973. *On the Technics and Politics of Transport Planning*. Institute of Urban and Regional Development, University of California at Berkeley, Working Paper no. 219.

Webber, Michael J. 1979. *Information Theory and Urban Spatial Structure*. London: Croom Helm.

Weber, Max. 1958. "Science as Vocation." In H. Greth and C. Wright Mills, eds., *From Max Weber*. New York: Oxford University Press.

Werkmeister, W. H. 1967. *Man and His Values*. Lincoln: University of Nebraska Press.

White, M., et al. 1980. *Managing Public Systems: Analytical Techniques for Public Administration*. North Scituate, Mass.: Duxbury Press.

Wiener, Norbert. 1961. *Cybernetics*. Cambridge, Mass.: MIT Press.

Williams, Fredrick. 1982. *The Communications Revolution*. New York: New American Library.

Williams, F., R. E. Rice, and E. M. Rogers, eds. 1988. *Research Methods and the New Media*. New York: Free Press.

Wingo, Lowdon. 1961. *Transportation and Land Use*. Washington, D.C.: Resources for the Future.

_____. 1963. "Urban Space in a Policy Perspective: An Introduction." In L. Wingo, ed., *Cities and Space*. Baltimore, Md.: Johns Hopkins University Press.

Winner, Langdon. 1977. *Autonomous Technology*. Cambridge, Mass.: MIT Press.

Wright, Frank Lloyd. 1958. *The Living City: When Democracy Builds*. New York: New American Library.

Wurster, Catherine. 1963. "The Form and Structure of the Future Urban Complex." In L. Wingo, ed., *Cities and Space*. Baltimore, Md.: Johns Hopkins University Press.

Wurtzel, Alan, and Colin Turner. 1977. "Latent Functions of the Telephone: What Missing the Extension Means." In Ithiel de Sola Pool, ed., *The Social Impact of the Telephone*. Boston, Mass.: MIT Press.

Index

About the Author

TARIK A. FATHY is President of T.H.E., Architects, Planners and Civil Engineers, Los Angeles Branch. He is also a partner at the T.H.E. Office for Architecture and Civil Design, Elmohandeseen, Egypt.